Experiencing the

Experiencing the Spirit

New Testament essentials
for every Christian

GRAHAM BEYNON

ivp

INTER-VARSITY PRESS
Norton Street, Nottingham NG7 3HR, England
Email: ivp@ivpbooks.com
Website: www.ivpbooks.com

First published 2006
Reprinted in this format 2010

British Library Cataloguing in Publication Data
A catalogue record for this book is available from the British Library.

ISBN: 978–1–84474–480–0

Set in Dante 10.5/13pt
Typeset in Great Britain by CRB Associates, Potterhanworth, Lincolnshire
Printed and bound in Great Britain by Ashford Colour Press Ltd, Gosport,
Hampshire

Inter-Varsity Press publishes Christian books that are true to the Bible and
that communicate the gospel, develop discipleship and strengthen the
church for its mission in the world.

Inter-Varsity Press is closely linked with the Universities and Colleges
Christian Fellowship, a student movement connecting Christian Unions
in universities and colleges throughout Great Britain, and a member
movement of the International Fellowship of Evangelical Students.
Website: www.uccf.org.uk

Contents

Preface

Knowing where and how a book started is often a helpful piece of information. The majority of these chapters first appeared as sermons preached at Knighton Evangelical Free Church and Avenue Community Church, both in Leicester. I preached them because I had a concern that we had a poor understanding of the work of the Spirit, myself included. I therefore set myself the task of preaching through a number of relevant passages.

The sermon series and this book were not supposed to be a comprehensive statement of all there is to say about the Spirit, but rather a good representation of who he is and especially what he does in our lives. Regarding the title of this book, I wanted to say something about what *experiencing* the Spirit is supposed to be like.

I have a lot of people to thank. First, those who read or heard the original sermons and fed back ideas and so enriched my thinking. Secondly, those who read a draft version of these chapters and provided a variety of comments. They were Orlando Saer, Anna Hartridge, Neil Powell and especially Ed Moll, who gave them more time and thought than they probably deserved.

Thirdly, thanks to my editor, Philip Duce, who encouraged me when I mentioned the idea of this book, and gave guidance and reassurance and his own helpful comments on drafts.

More generally I owe a debt to all those I've read and heard on this topic. I'm not a particularly original thinker and in my speaking and writing I constantly look around me for inspiration and ideas. As a result, the thinking, explanations and illustrations of many others are contained in these chapters. You can be sure the best moments are not my own, but all the inadequacies most certainly are.

My wife, Charis, and I would like to dedicate this book to our children, Cara, Isaac and Jed, in the prayerful hope that they too will experience the wonderful work of God's Spirit in their lives.

Graham Beynon

The big sister?

My wife, Charis, was once trying to explain who the Holy Spirit is to our children. They'd got hold of the idea of God the Father and they didn't have a problem with Jesus as God's Son, but they were struggling with the Spirit. In a slight moment of desperation Charis decided to push the 'family' picture a bit further. 'We've got the Father and the Son,' she said, 'so the Spirit is a bit like the big sister.' The children weren't so sure and were subsequently sent to talk to their dad.

That exchange illustrates the difficulty many of us have with the Holy Spirit. We know he exists, we know we should believe in him, and we're sure he's important, but he remains something of a mystery. As a result, some Christians have stayed rather quiet about the Spirit – we're not too sure what to say about him.

Others, of course, speak with great confidence and enthusiasm about the Spirit. We are challenged to be 'open to the Spirit' or to live a 'Spirit-filled life', or asked whether we know the 'empowering of the Spirit'. All of this sounds either exciting or scary, depending on our background, personality and a whole variety of other factors. Because of this, the Spirit has sometimes been a source of controversy, with some people feeling he is like the awkward family relative we don't mention because to do so would be to open up a can of worms we can't handle.

At one level it's easy to say who the Holy Spirit is. Look in any theology book and it will tell you he is the 'third member of the Trinity'. That's not the most helpful of definitions, but it does tell us some important stuff. It reminds us that God is a tri-unity. The Godhead is made up of three distinct persons who are equally divine and are utterly united in love and purpose. So God is a relational, personal God even within himself – not a solitary being who is alone in the universe and looking for friends.

But being a trinity doesn't just mean God is relational within himself; it also relates to how God 'works'. The three persons in the Godhead are not only distinct persons; they also have distinct roles. So it is the Father who initiates and rules – this is why Jesus says he is dependent on him and can do only what the Father does (see John 5:19). And then it is through the Son that the Father acts. So, for example, it is through Jesus that the world is created, that rule and judgment are exercised, and that salvation is achieved.

But what about the Spirit? What is the Spirit's role? That is the subject of this book. I need to warn you that because we are dealing with how God works in the world our topic is very broad. The Spirit has a role in all that God does and so we could discuss virtually everything. We'll look at the main passages in which the Spirit's work is described in the New Testament. My aim in doing so is to try to build a picture of what the Spirit does, and so of what experiencing the work of the Spirit in our lives should look like for us.

1: New life in the Spirit

John 3:1–8

A friend and I used go hitchhiking together. Whenever we got a lift I would slump back in my seat and relax to enjoy the ride. My friend Martin, however, would always feel the need to start a conversation with whomever was kindly giving us a lift. Having jumped into one car, he leant forward from the back seat to talk to the driver and his companion in the front.

His opening gambit ran: 'Nice car, this.'

'Hmm,' said the driver.

Martin tried again. 'Nice and fast, not like our last lift. Really slow, that was.' (Our previous driver had insisted on driving at about 25 miles per hour.)

'Oh,' said the driver.

Undaunted, Martin pressed on. 'And we had a really heavy conversation with the last guy as well.' (We'd mentioned being Christians to our previous driver, but he had responded with his philosophy of life, which seemed to revolve mainly around organic vegetables.)

'Oh,' said our driver. Then he finally responded: 'He wasn't one of those born-again Christians, was he?'

Martin beamed. 'No,' he said, 'but we are.'

I still smile at the memory of that. But I also wince at the memory of the tone of voice with which that driver asked his question. The phrase 'born-again Christian' was uttered, not with venom, but with an unmistakable mocking tone. If the answer from us had been, 'Yes, he was one of those born-again Christians', no doubt the conversation would have turned to laughter at such silly people who believe such ridiculous ideas.

The term 'born-again Christian' conjures up a variety of images. It might be the American TV evangelist in his shiny suit. Or the preacher on the street corner, calling out, 'You must be born again.' Or the mocking newspaper article about a celebrity: Britney Spears becomes a born-again Christian! Whatever the precise image is that may come to mind, the connotations aren't usually good ones.

As a result, some today within the church want to avoid this term, or at least rethink the whole concept of being born again. We'll think about that at the end of this chapter. First, we need to look at what Jesus said about it.

Jesus on being born again

Jesus uses this term in a conversation with a Pharisee. We read about it in John's gospel:

> Now there was a Pharisee named Nicodemus, a member of the Jewish ruling council. He came to Jesus at night and said, 'Rabbi, we know that you are a teacher who has come from God. For you could not perform the signs you are doing if God were not with you.'
>
> In reply Jesus declared, 'I tell you the truth, no-one can see the kingdom of God without being born again.'
>
> 'How can anyone be born in old age?' Nicodemus asked. 'Surely they cannot enter a second time into their mother's womb to be born!'

Jesus answered, 'I tell you the truth, no-one can enter the kingdom of God without being born of water and the Spirit. Flesh gives birth to flesh, but the Spirit gives birth to spirit. You should not be surprised at my saying, "You must be born again." The wind blows wherever it pleases. You hear its sound, but you cannot tell where it comes from or where it is going. So it is with everyone born of the Spirit.' (John 3:1–8)

Nicodemus is interested in Jesus. He recognizes there's some- thing special about him because of the miraculous signs he's been doing, and it looks as if he's come to find out more. We don't really know what his exact question is, though, because Jesus doesn't give him a chance to ask it. Instead, Jesus simply replies by saying that no-one can see the kingdom of God unless he is born again.

Nicodemus, however, doesn't seem to understand, and asks how that could ever work. So Jesus says it again but slightly differently in verse 5: no-one can enter the kingdom of God unless they are born of water and the Spirit. So we have two statements of Jesus on this which we can put side by side:

- No-one can see the kingdom of God without being born again (verse 3).
- No-one can enter the kingdom of God without being born of water and the Spirit (verse 5).

Seeing the kingdom and entering the kingdom are really two ways of saying the same thing. They both refer to being in the kingdom. 'Seeing' the kingdom means 'experiencing' it. For example, later in the gospel Jesus speaks about 'seeing life', meaning experiencing life personally, not seeing it with your eyes.

We need to think about the different elements of these state- ments. What did Jesus mean by the kingdom of God, and what is this new birth needed to get into it?

The kingdom of God

You know the 'Which side are you on?' stuff in films. In *Star Wars* it's 'Which side of the force are you on?' In *The Lord of the Rings* it's 'Are you with the king or with Sauron?' There are two forces battling against each other and you are on one side or the other.

Jesus says there is a spiritual equivalent to do with God: there is the kingdom of God and there is the kingdom of darkness. And you are in one or the other. You're either in God's kingdom or you're fighting against him. You're his subject, or you're a rebel. So what Jesus is talking about here when he speaks about being in the kingdom of God is about being under the rule of God, being on God's side, rather than being his enemy.

Now Nicodemus, as a Pharisee, would have known that God was going to bring his rule, his kingdom, in a new way in the world. The Old Testament looked forward to such a time, when God would be seen to be king and his rule would hold sway. Pharisees like him looked forward to such a day. And he would have expected that he would be included in this kingdom automatically. He presumed he was on God's side, and when the kingdom came he'd be one of the subjects. After all, he was strict in his obedience, pious in his religion and conservative in his theology. Surely he was on God's side already.

But Jesus shoots down all his assumptions. To be in the kingdom, to be on God's side, Jesus says, you must be born again. In fact, Jesus stresses the absolute necessity of it. No-one, he says, can see the kingdom and no-one can enter the kingdom without this experience of new life. This might help us see why Jesus doesn't even let Nicodemus ask his question. He has come to Jesus assuming that he's on God's side already, and wants to see what Jesus can add to his knowledge. Jesus, however, stops him in his tracks. He wants to make it clear that Nicodemus can make no assumptions, and indeed cannot consider himself under God's rule unless this dramatic change of being 'born again' takes place.

Being born again

So what does he mean by 'born again'? Well, first of all, we need to notice that the term Jesus uses can mean either 'born *again*' or 'born *from above*'. Later in this passage, in verse 31, Jesus uses the same word when he talks about himself as the one who has come down 'from above'. So people have debated which way it should be translated, and most Bibles have a footnote with the alternative rendering. Actually, I think we'll see that Jesus chooses this word deliberately to convey both ideas.

Secondly, we need to look at the phrase 'born of water and the Spirit'. That phrase has also been taken in different ways. Some have suggested it means born physically (which, as anyone present at a birth can tell you, involves a variety of fluids – which could be referred to as 'water') and then by the Spirit. Others have suggested it means 'baptized in water and born again by the Spirit'.

Both of those are possible, but we should notice that in verse 10 Jesus seems to think that Nicodemus should understand this stuff: 'You are Israel's teacher, and do you not understand these things?' That comment suggests that the answer to this idea is to be found in the Old Testament. Nicodemus, as a teacher of the Old Testament, should have known better.

A number of Old Testament passages looked forward to a time when God would work by his Spirit in a new way. For example, Joel chapter 2 talks about God pouring out his Spirit on all people. The most important of these references, however, is from Ezekiel 36, because it mentions not only the Spirit but also water:

'I will sprinkle clean water on you, and you will be clean; I will cleanse you from all your impurities and from all your idols. I will give you a new heart and put a new spirit in you; I will remove from you your heart of stone and give you a heart of flesh. And I will put my Spirit in you and move you to follow my decrees and be careful to keep my laws.'
(Ezekiel 36:25–27)

You can see the idea of being washed clean by water and being renewed in some way by the Spirit, which fits with this idea of 'new birth' that Jesus is talking about. And that passage in Ezekiel is followed by Ezekiel's famous vision of a valley of dry bones in chapter 37. Ezekiel sees what is basically a pile of skeletons. And he is told to prophesy to them, and as he does so God's Spirit comes and makes them alive. God says in that passage, 'I will put my Spirit in you and you will live.' That's the background Jesus has in mind when he speaks about being born again.

Spiritual corpses

This is a view of people that thinks of them as spiritually dead, or as spiritual corpses. If you have ever seen one of those horror films where you have zombies walking around, you've got a picture of the 'living dead'. They are alive in a sense, but not properly alive. That's what Jesus is saying we're like. We are alive physically, but spiritually we're dead. There's a whole side to us missing.

This takes us right back to what God said in the Garden of Eden. God told Adam that they must not eat from the tree of the knowledge of good and evil. His warning was: 'When you eat of it you will surely die' (Genesis 2:17). But when Adam and Eve ate from it, they didn't die physically on that day. Physical death came later, but the significant thing that happened that day was that they were put out of the garden. Or we could say they were put out of God's kingdom. On that day they died spiritually. Their relationship with God as their father and king ended.

And that's our situation – we are spiritual corpses. That is our problem. And because that's our problem we can see what the solution is. Jesus doesn't come to give us a moral reform programme; he doesn't come to tell us about religious practice. None of that will help when you're a spiritual corpse. What we need is *new life* – we need to be born again.

Re-creation

We need God to work by his Spirit in us, to re-create that spiritual part of us that has died. That is what Jesus is talking about here. This is the 'new life' we need. Later in John's gospel Jesus gives us a definition of this life. He says, 'Now this is eternal life: that they may know you, the only true God, and Jesus Christ, whom you have sent' (John 17:3). True life is about knowing God; it means a relationship with God which has been lost in spiritual death and can be regained only by spiritual birth – being 'born again'.

This is why I think Jesus chose a word that had two shades of meaning. We could translate it 'born again' because it is about a new life. We could translate it 'born from above' because it is about God working to give us a new life. I think Jesus wanted to convey both those ideas. It is a new life, but it's not just us turning over a new leaf; it is new life coming from outside ourselves. It comes from above, from God himself.

This idea of being re-created to know God, being born again, is a truth that is repeated in the rest of the New Testament.

As for you, you were dead in your transgressions and sins . . . [God] made us alive with Christ even when we were dead.
(Ephesians 2:1, 5)

He saved us through the washing of rebirth and renewal by the Holy Spirit.
(Titus 3:5)

If anyone is in Christ, there is a new creation.
(2 Corinthians 5:17)

Here is an incredible truth. We are re-created by God's Spirit. The Holy Spirit is the one who brings life. It's as though God breathes his Spirit into us to resuscitate us. Or the Holy Spirit comes and brings that divine shock that gets our spiritual heart beating again. We move from death to life. Part of us is re-created by God.

Thinking about becoming a Christian

I mentioned earlier that some people say we need to rethink what being born again means. The suggestions vary, but include things like 'turning over a new leaf with God', or 'deciding to adopt Jesus' new agenda'. But those sorts of suggestion don't deal with all we've discussed above. What they actually do is play down the change that happens when someone becomes a Christian. They make that change more respectable! The reality is very humbling for us. We don't simply need to turn over a new leaf with God; we need to be given new life! We don't just need to adopt a new agenda; we need God to re-create us because we're dead. That's how bad it is, and so that's what we need.

Realize the change needed

How would you describe yourself before becoming a Christian? We all have different pasts, so some would speak of a wild life apart from God, while others would say they were just average people. But the biblical description includes stuff like 'dead to God', 'enemies of God', 'lovers of sin'. For example, in Titus 3:3 Paul describes himself and everyone else like this: 'At one time we too were foolish, disobedient, deceived and enslaved by all kinds of passions and pleasures. We lived in malice and envy, being hated and hating one another.'

And he goes on to say that God saved us because of his mercy by the washing of rebirth and renewal by the Holy Spirit. That's humbling, isn't it – to be told the situation was so bad we needed a new heart; we couldn't just clean up the old one? We were dead to God and needed him to remake us. We were living a life enslaved to sin and needed him to wash us and renew us by his Spirit.

We mustn't play down the change involved in becoming a Christian. Rather, we need to play it up, because we are all prone to forgetting the depth of change needed. We are all prone to thinking God just needed to dust us off, rather than raise us from the dead. And, of course, if we realize this, we go on to thank God for his mercy and to rejoice in his remaking us. This results in great humility and great gratitude.

Realize that the change is needed by all

This might sound obvious, but we also need to remember that this is the change everyone needs. Remember, Jesus said that 'no-one' could enter the kingdom without the Spirit renewing them in this way.

There was a famous evangelist in the eighteenth century called George Whitefield, who kept on speaking from John 3. Someone once asked him why he kept on preaching on this text and saying 'You must be born again'. He replied, 'Because, sir, you *must* be born again.' This is a necessity for everyone.

In other words, there is only one kind of Christian in the world – the born-again kind. It doesn't matter what background we're from, what we have or haven't done, what skeletons there are or aren't in the cupboard. We *all* needed God to work a miracle in us and give us new life.

We can get into thinking that some people are so nice and pleasant that God doesn't have to do very much to them for them to become Christians, and meanwhile others are so bad that it's a real overhaul job for God. In other words, we start to grade people. The biblical grading, however, is very simple: everyone is dead spiritually, and everyone needs this miracle of new life.

And so there is only one type of Christian. That is a great leveller among us. That means I can never start to look down on other Christians, thinking to myself, 'They are lucky: God renewed them.' I was just as dead as they were, and they are now just as much alive by the Spirit as I am. Equally, God hasn't made some people more 'alive' than others. There can be no grading systems in the church!

Realize that the change can look different

While this regeneration by the Spirit is the experience we all need, we must realize that it can look very different for different people.

In some groups, being born again has been presented as a stereotyped experience: usually as a crisis moment when you finally 'pray the prayer' for forgiveness. As a result, you can date and time your new birth. In fact, I'm told you can get 'New Birth' certificates to keep with your original birth certificate. On this certificate you put the date and time and place of being born again. But that rather presumes you know the details!

Some people, of course, do know the details. They can talk you through the event; they can give you the precise timing; they fit the stereotype. But for others it looks very different. I became a Christian between the ages of seventeen and eighteen, but I can't tell you exactly when. That year was something of a journey of discovery. I gradually came to understand the truth of the gospel. By the end of the year I'd understood the gospel and I trusted Jesus' death for me. But I can't date it any more precisely than that, and there was no 'crisis' on the way. And, of course, for many people, especially those who have grown up in a Christian family, they may be very unclear when this new birth happened.

The problem comes when we start to be prescriptive of what it must look like. Sometimes those who've had the 'crisis' conversion can suggest that unless you too can date and time your new birth, it hasn't really happened. That's really unhelpful and undermining of other people's experience.

Many have used the illustration of a journey, say on a train, where you are unsure when you crossed a certain bridge. The important thing is to know that you have crossed it – you are on the other side; you do have this new life in the Spirit. How can we know? We'll think about that a little below. The important thing for now is to say that while we all need this rebirth we mustn't prescribe what it looks like.

Should I call myself a 'born-again Christian'?

I was getting to know a student called Luke. He was interested in Christianity and we were about to start some Bible studies

2

together for him to discover more about Jesus. Before we began, though, he said he had a question for me. I wondered what was coming.

'Are you a born-again Christian?' he asked.

The way he asked the question made it sound as if saying 'Yes' would be the wrong answer in his book. In fact, his tone of voice suggested that if I dared say 'Yes', the Bible studies together would be off.

Presumably that was because of all the baggage that the term 'born again' can have. So should I disown the term and say, 'No, don't worry, I'm not weird like that lot'? But what about being prepared to be scorned as a Christian? What if he did understand what born again really meant and he simply didn't want anything to do with real Christianity?

Those were the thoughts that were running through my mind at that moment – or at least something along those lines. And they simply show that whether we use the term or not all depends on whom we are talking to and what they understand by it. For many people it is so loaded with unhelpful connotations we're best off avoiding it. However, we mustn't start to become embarrassed about what Jesus actually meant as if we had to apologize for him. Indeed, as we've said above, we want to argue that, properly understood, there is only one kind of Christian – the born-again kind.

So what I actually said to Luke was something like this. 'Yes, I am, but I'd want a moment to explain what I think Jesus meant by that.'

'Fair enough,' he replied.

We then discussed some of the stuff in this chapter. At the end of that he might still have decided I was weird and he didn't want to find out any more – but at least he'd have been reacting against the real thing rather than the stereotype. As it happens, he did find out more and was born again himself a few weeks later.

Thinking about living as a Christian

This truth also gives me a perspective on my life as a Christian. Being a Christian is not just about having a new status but rather about having a new life. As a Christian I'm not simply forgiven and justified – although of course I am, and that is wonderful. But it's not that I've booked my place in heaven and now I simply wait for it to arrive. It's not that I breathe a sigh of relief that I'm OK with God now and then get on with my life. It's not even that I get on with life, making changes to show how grateful I am to God.

The truth is that, as well as a change of status with God, there is a change in me! I've been re-created. I've been born again and so now I live a new life. I've entered the kingdom and now I start to live life in the kingdom. That's the new life in the Spirit that this book tries to explore.

It's a life where the Spirit brings me to trust Jesus and grow to know him as my Saviour and Lord. It's a life where I can know God and grow in relationship with him as my Father. It's a life where the Spirit leads me and empowers me to change and live to serve God. Being born again marks the start of a whole new life.

For example, the apostle John later writes in one of his letters about those who are born of God, those who have this new life. He says that this new life will show itself in our belief and trust in Jesus as our Saviour, in loving God, in loving each other, and in hating and fighting sin. (See, for example, 1 John 3:9–10; 4:7–8; 5:1.)

Spot the difference

In other words, being born again means that becoming a Christian is to start a new life which then shows itself. So while the experience of being born again may look different among us, the new life we live should be very similar. We should each be showing faith in Jesus, a growing relationship with God, love for each other and so on. They are signs of new life.

And this is why we should rightly be suspicious of those who claim to be born again but then don't show new life. Most famously, Larry Flynt, who publishes pornographic magazines in the USA, became a born-again Christian. And having been born again, he carried on publishing his magazines. I think it's OK to say he's probably not born again. That, unfortunately, is often the case with 'celebrity' conversions. Equally unfortunate is that it can be the case with non-celebrities as well – our friends and family. We need to be careful in making any such judgments, of course; sometimes they can be very hard to make. But the point is simply that new life should show itself. The challenge for us is to ask how much we are showing this new life ourselves. That's what this book tries to lead us through.

study 1

John 3:1–8

1. What do you think was in Nicodemus' mind as he came to speak to Jesus?
2. Try to put Jesus' answer in verse 3 and verse 5 into your own words. How should Nicodemus have understood it?
3. How does verse 6 help us understand what Jesus is saying? What does it mean we are missing in our lives?
4. Jesus' comments about needing to be born again suggest that in some sense we need new life. In what way is that true of us?
5. How does Jesus' teaching on the need to be born again mean we should think about ourselves? What attitude should it result in?
6. What dangers do we face if we don't emphasize the need to be 'born again' as Jesus does?
7. How should we react when our culture caricatures and misunderstands the idea of being 'born again'?
8. What does experiencing the work of the Holy Spirit involve, according to this passage?

2: Knowing Jesus by the Spirit

John 16:5-16

> Shirley and I personally invite you to join us for our Holy
> Land Experience ... In all our years of ministry, nothing has
> been more meaningful or had more spiritual impact than
> touring the Holy Land ... we walk in the footsteps of Jesus
> and see the pages of the Bible come to life.

So runs a standard advert for a trip to tour round Israel. It sounds
appealing, doesn't it? Not just as a holiday but as a spiritual
experience. The standard phrase used of such trips is that they will
bring Jesus and/or the Bible 'to life'. In fact, if you can't go on the
trip you can buy one of numerous DVDs and see Jesus/the Bible
'come to life' in your front room. Bringing something to life, of
course, makes it sound as if our current experience might be, well,
dead.

That sort of stuff shows that we can feel a distance between
ourselves and Jesus. We'd like to bridge that gap; we want him to
become more real to us. Ultimately I guess we'd say we wanted
to have lived 2,000 years ago in the Middle East so that we
could have actually met Jesus. We could have seen him with

our own eyes and heard him with our own ears – seen a miracle, heard some teaching. Maybe we'd have even sat and shared a meal with him. Just imagine the effect that would have. Wouldn't *that* bring Jesus to life a little more? Make him a bit more real to us?

I can imagine that a non-Christian who is sceptical about Jesus might say, 'If only I'd met him, then I might believe in him.' And equally I can imagine that a Christian, who does believe, might say, 'If only I'd met him, then I would *really* know him. I'd have had a personal knowledge of him.' Wouldn't it have been good if we had all had the chance to meet Jesus? We might even think to ourselves at this moment, 'What a shame we didn't get the chance. If only Jesus had never left this earth. If only he'd stayed here with us. Surely then people would believe in him; surely then we'd really know him.'

Well, it's time to stop such thoughts because Jesus has something to tell us in verse 7 of John 16:

'I tell you the truth: It is for your good that I am going away. Unless I go away, the Counsellor will not come to you; but if I go, I will send him to you.'

The disciples' thoughts weren't the same as ours because they *had* met Jesus in the flesh. But they didn't want him to leave either. They were full of grief at the very idea of losing him and worried that all they would be left with was memories of Jesus. And, as important as memories are, they are only memories, not a continuation of the relationship. They too would say, 'Surely it would be better if you stayed, Jesus.'

But Jesus disagrees. 'It is for your good that I am going away,' he says. And the reason for this, of course, is the Holy Spirit. The remarkable thing we have to see in these words is that Jesus thinks it is better that we lose him, so that we can gain the Counsellor, the Holy Spirit. And what we need to do is to think about why that is; why that exchange is a good one as far as

Jesus is concerned, when it runs against the thoughts we started with.

The answer to this question lies in who the Holy Spirit is and what the Holy Spirit does. We'll think about those in turn.

Who the Holy Spirit is

In the verse quoted above, Jesus calls the Holy Spirit 'the Counsellor'. He's picking up on what he said back in John 14:16–17: 'I will ask the Father, and he will give you another Counsellor to be with you for ever – the Spirit of truth.'

Jesus says the Holy Spirit is 'another Counsellor'. There's a lot in that phrase. First, that means the Holy Spirit is a *person*, because the word 'counsellor' always referred to a person. And Jesus refers to him as a 'he', not an 'it'.

We need to note that fact, because we can easily slip into thinking of the Holy Spirit as an energy, or a force, as if he's some sort of divine electricity. And some passages in the Bible might lead us to think like that – the Holy Spirit coming to empower someone, for example. But he's not a power we experience; he is a person we know. And in a moment we'll see why that's so important.

Secondly, he is a *helper*. I think that's a better word than 'counsellor', because today to call someone a 'counsellor' sounds as if he might sit you on a couch and ask you about your childhood. But the word Jesus uses has the idea of someone who is called alongside, to assist you or help you. This is why some translations put it as 'another Advocate', because it could be used for someone who would assist you in court, someone who would speak in your defence. We'll come back to that in a moment in looking at what the Spirit does.

This leads us to the third thing, which is that the Spirit is like *another Jesus*. When Jesus calls him 'another Counsellor', or another helper, that means there must have been a previous one.

And that was Jesus himself. And the word Jesus uses when he says 'another Counsellor' means 'another of the same kind', rather than one that is different. So Jesus is promising a kind of replacement.

We can put that together with Jesus' various promises to return to be with his disciples. For example, see how he puts it in 14:18: 'I will not leave you as orphans; I will come to you.' Some people have thought Jesus means there that he'll come back after the cross in the resurrection and so be with his disciples again. But of course he would return in that way only for a month or so before he left again. So there's not a lot of consolation there for the disciples; they would be left as orphans eventually. Instead, he must mean, 'I will come back to you and be with you in the person of the Holy Spirit.' And so the Spirit is like another 'me'.

Let me illustrate it. I've got an identical twin brother. We really are very alike, not only in appearance, but also, so people say, in our mannerisms and expressions. When we visit each other, all kinds of confusion are caused among friends we meet! Now, if I were leaving my church, I could say to the congregation, 'I'm going, but I'll send another Graham.' Obviously they might like to ask for something different, but you see the point. I could promise another one just like me, to take my place.

That's what Jesus is promising here – another helper to be with them, to take his place. The Holy Spirit and Jesus are so similar that Jesus can speak about coming to them, or later he can say he'll be with them for ever (Matthew 28:20). We can see this close identification again in Paul's letter to the Romans: 'The *Spirit of God* lives in you. And if anyone does not have the *Spirit of Christ*, he does not belong to Christ. But if *Christ* is in you . . .' (8:9–10).

Paul refers to the Spirit of God, to the Spirit of Christ and to Christ himself living in them. These are all different ways of speaking about the Holy Spirit, because he is so like Jesus. In fact, it's not only that they are so similar; this is closely tied to our second point, which concerns what the Spirit does.

What the Holy Spirit does

The Holy Spirit is like 'another' Jesus coming, not only because he is so like Jesus, but also because his work is *to show Jesus to us*, or to make Jesus real to us. We mentioned above that the Spirit was an advocate who would speak for Jesus. In Jesus' day, you didn't have defence lawyers. Instead, you had witnesses who came forward to speak in your defence. They did so simply by giving their evidence; they spoke the truth about you to vindicate you. That's what the Holy Spirit comes to do with Jesus. He bears witness to him, and speaks the truth about him. We see this most clearly back in chapter 16 of John's Gospel, where Jesus talks about what the Spirit will do when he comes.

He brings us to believe
There are two parts to this showing us Jesus. First, he brings us to believe in Jesus. See John 16:8–11:

> 'When he comes, he will convict the world of guilt in regard to sin and righteousness and judgment: in regard to sin, because people do not believe in me; in regard to righteousness, because I am going to the Father, where you can see me no longer; and in regard to judgment, because the prince of this world now stands condemned.'

The Holy Spirit convinces people. He gets people to change their minds and see things differently. And Jesus gives us three areas in which he brings this new conviction – sin, righteousness and judgment – and he gives us a reason for each one. First, there needs to be conviction in regard to sin, because people don't believe in Jesus. The Holy Spirit will bring people to understand that they've rejected God; in particular, they'll see that they've rejected Jesus. They'll come to see that they stand guilty of not believing in him when they should.

Secondly, there needs to be conviction in regard to right-eousness because Jesus is going to the Father. This is a more debated phrase and it's not immediately clear what Jesus means. I think it's talking about the righteousness of Jesus and saying that people will come to understand that Jesus was right in all he said and did. The Spirit will have to do this because Jesus himself is not there to show it for himself any more; he is going to the Father.

Thirdly, there needs to be conviction in regard to judgment because the prince of this world now stands condemned. That is, the Holy Spirit will bring people to see the certainty of judgment for all those who would side with the devil, that is, against God. He'll do that because through Jesus the devil is condemned already.

The bottom line is this: people who'd say they've done nothing wrong and have no concern about God will change their minds because of the Holy Spirit going to work on them. People who'd say Jesus is of no relevance to them, and they have no need of him, will be convinced otherwise. People who didn't understand a thing about Jesus will see the truth of who he is and what he's done. The Holy Spirit will bring people to believe in Jesus.

Have you ever tried to take a photo and the flash hasn't worked? You end up with a pretty dark picture. You usually can't see who's in it or what they're doing. If you take the same shot again with the flash, suddenly everything becomes clear. Think of the Holy Spirit as like a light who shines on Jesus, so that we can see him clearly – so that we can see him for who he truly is, and understand what it is he's done. The Holy Spirit shines his light so that we're convinced of these things, so that we come to believe.

This work of the Holy Spirit is repeated and explained further in the rest of the New Testament. 'No-one can say, "Jesus is Lord," except by the Holy Spirit', Paul tells us (1 Corinthians 12:3). In other words, you need the Holy Spirit to work in you so that you understand that Jesus is Lord and confess it for yourself; otherwise Jesus stays in the dark.

Or look at these words from 2 Corinthians 4:6: 'For God, who said, "Let light shine out of darkness," made his light shine in our hearts to give us the light of the knowledge of the glory of God in the face of Christ.' It's condensed language, but the idea is this: God shines his light so that we can know that God is glorious in Jesus. We can come to see that what God has done in Jesus is so great. That's the work of the Holy Spirit showing us Jesus so we believe in him.

So if you are someone who believes in Jesus, it is because the Holy Spirit has come and he has convinced you of these things. He has worked his stuff in your heart and mind. You haven't simply decided to think differently; you haven't worked it all out by yourself. God has worked in you to show you Jesus.

This is an encouragement to us in trying to convince others of the truth about Jesus. I wonder if you despair sometimes that no-one will ever come to believe what you believe about Jesus – maybe a member of your family, a colleague at work, or a long-standing friend or neighbour. It can look unlikely sometimes because people can be so uninterested and so unconvinced. Our explanations and arguments can seem like water off a duck's back. Nothing gets through. We mustn't lose heart, because there's someone working on the inside – the Spirit. He will use our words and explanations, so we mustn't stop giving them. But he is the one who will work to bring interest instead of dismissal, and conviction instead of unbelief.

Come back to Jesus' words that we started with: 'It is for your good that I am going away.' Jesus says that even if he were here himself, he would not lead people to believe with any more certainty than the invisible work of conviction that the Holy Spirit is doing. In fact, Jesus says it's better that he left, and we don't see him, so that the Holy Spirit will come and do that in us and in others.

He brings us to know

Believing in Jesus is one part of the Spirit showing us Jesus. But there's a second part: he brings us to know Jesus. Back to John 16, and verses 12–13:

'I have much more to say to you, more than you can now bear. But when he, the Spirit of truth, comes, he will guide you into all truth. He will not speak on his own; he will speak only what he hears, and he will tell you what is yet to come.'

Jesus couldn't tell the disciples all he wanted to tell them there and then because they couldn't take it all in. There was just too much to say. So the Holy Spirit would teach them; he would guide them into all truth. When he says 'all truth' there, he means all the truth he wants them to have – what he would have taught them himself if they could have handled it.

This truth that the Holy Spirit will teach is truth specifically about Jesus. Following on in chapter 16, verses 14–15:

'He will bring glory to me by taking from what is mine and making it known to you. All that belongs to the Father is mine. That is why I said the Spirit will take from what is mine and make it known to you.'

The Spirit would take all that is true of Jesus, all that Jesus is, all that he's done, and make it known to them. And so the Spirit would glorify Jesus by leading people to know him, to understand him.

I remember seeing the opening ceremony of the 2004 Olympics. It was one of those impressive but rather peculiar displays. Strange symbols and shapes were unfurled; there were patterns and colours that obviously meant something, but it wasn't at all clear what. However, the TV presenters had obviously been given some kind of crib that explained each part, because, as the display unfolded, they explained what was going on and what it represented. We needed them to give that explanation; otherwise we wouldn't have understood all we were supposed to.

It's the same idea here. The Holy Spirit gives the explanation about Jesus; he makes the truth about Jesus known to the disciples. They needed someone to come and explain more fully all that they'd seen of Jesus, and all that they'd heard. They needed to be guided into the truth about Jesus, because they wouldn't get there by themselves.

Now, it has to be said that these verses have been badly abused. One friend of mine told me that ideally he would have no need of the Bible in his Christian life; he'd have no need ever to read it. When I asked him why, he said it was because he had the Holy Spirit, who would guide him into all truth. He thought the Bible was a prop for those who didn't listen to the Spirit very well.

But Jesus isn't promising a direct download of truth to each and every Christian. We need to remember he's speaking here to the apostles, who have a special role in revealing truth. Back in chapter 14 he says the Holy Spirit will teach them and *remind* them of everything he'd said (14:26). Clearly, 'reminding' can happen only for those who heard it in the first place.

Jesus is saying that the apostles would have this reminder by the Spirit and further teaching by the Spirit so that they would be led into 'all truth'. This is why their sermons and thinking went into the Bible. And that is why our sermons and thinking should come out of the Bible. The truth they were given is now in our hands when we open the Bible. But the Holy Spirit is still involved in leading *us* into the truth, because we still need the Holy Spirit to work if we are to understand this truth and to know Jesus.

Let me try an illustration. Think of a stained-glass window and imagine that the window gives us the truth about Jesus. All that he is, all that he's done – imagine it could all be contained in that picture. Well, it is as if the apostles were led to put that window together. The Holy Spirit reminded them of the teaching Jesus had given them, gave them further insight into it and so guided them into the truth about Jesus. He made it known to them so that they could present the true picture to everyone else.

We now look at that window, at that presentation of Jesus, in the Bible. But for us to see anything in a stained-glass window we not only need it to be put together, we also need light shining through it. If there isn't any light shining through, we see nothing.

That's what it's like here with the Holy Spirit bringing us to know Jesus. First, he leads the apostles into all truth, which they write down for us. But then the Spirit must shine through for us to see the picture clearly. So the sixteenth-century reformer John Calvin once wrote that 'God does not bestow the Spirit on his people, in order to set aside the use of his word, but rather to render it fruitful.' (We're going to think more about the role of Holy Spirit and the Bible in a later chapter.)

And the result is the same for them and for us: the Spirit brings us to know Jesus – not just to believe in him, but to know him. We saw earlier that the Spirit is like another Jesus with us, so it's as though Jesus himself is with us. This is how that works: the Spirit shows us the truth about Jesus; he makes Jesus known to us; he makes him real to us.

Knowing a person

Some people have often spoken of knowing Jesus as if he were a historical figure you learn facts about. The important thing, they say, is that we know the truth about him. As a result, this group is often very concerned with careful formulations of that truth, so that we have our understanding of Jesus spot on. Meanwhile, others have spoken of knowing Jesus as if it were a mystical personal experience that they can't describe. The important thing, they say, is that they have experienced him. And as a result they often haven't been so concerned about pinning it down very precisely.

The first group focuses on the facts – but knowing facts about a historical person doesn't mean there is a living relationship. The second group focuses on the experience – but an experience without any solid information has no substance or certainty to it.

But here, with Jesus and the Spirit, you have both these elements. This knowing of Jesus involves knowing truth about him – it comes from the Spirit of truth. And so this involves knowledge you can reason over and explain. In other words, this has very clear content. You can pin it down; you can and you should discuss it. It's perfectly possible to be wrong about it and to need to be corrected on it. It involves knowing truth.

But it is truth of a person, Jesus, brought to you by a person, the Holy Spirit, and so this truth involves a relationship. This involves an experience of that person, just as any real relationship does. And so we should expect knowing Jesus to be an experience, rather than an academic study of a historical person. Sometimes you learn so much about someone that you might say, 'I feel like I almost know them.' But of course you really only know *about* them. But not with Jesus – we have his Spirit in us, making him real to us.

We need to keep both of these elements together. A church that emphasizes an experience of the Spirit without truth about Jesus is full only of hot air. But a church that emphasizes truth about Jesus without an experience of him by the Spirit is dead.

The Spirit and Jesus

So who is the Holy Spirit? He's like another Jesus. And what does he do? He shows us Jesus. He brings us to believe in him and know him. Do you see what this means? This means you and I can know Jesus Christ personally; we can have a relationship with him. In this, Christianity is unique. Other religions don't claim anything like this. With the prophet Muhammad, or the Buddha, people follow their teachings, they respect and revere their example, but they don't claim to know them as a person or have a relationship with him. How could they? They're in the wrong place at the wrong time. Well, we're too late to meet Jesus ourselves in the flesh. But Jesus says we can meet him by his Spirit. In fact, he says it's better that he leaves, *so that* we can meet him by his Spirit.

Imagine being given the following choice. You can sit on the Mount of Olives and see Jesus with your own two eyes and hear Jesus teach with your own two ears. Or you can sit at home, or at church, with the Bible in your hand and the Spirit in your heart. Which would you choose? Jesus says that if we are wise we will choose the latter.

I don't know about you, but that really encourages me to grow to know Jesus. That means I want to pick up my Bible tomorrow morning and read it. That means I want to live tomorrow conscious of Jesus. That means I want to grow in my walk with Jesus. Because it is real. The Holy Spirit makes it so.

study 2

John 14:16–21; 16:7–15

Read John 14:16–21

1. Jesus calls the Holy Spirit 'another Counsellor'. What do we learn about the Holy Spirit from this phrase?
2. What is the difference between the world's experience of the Spirit and the believer's experience of the Spirit from these verses? Why?
3. Jesus is reassuring his disciples about his leaving them. In what way is his teaching about the Spirit reassuring?

Read John 16:7–15

4. What three things will the Holy Spirit do in the world when Jesus sends him? Discuss the brief explanation Jesus gives for each one.
5. What will the Holy Spirit do for the apostles in particular when Jesus sends him? How does this benefit us today?
6. What does verse 14 tell us about the Holy Spirit's work? What does that mean the work of the Spirit will look like in someone's life?
7. Why does all of this mean it is better if Jesus leaves so the Spirit can come (verse 7)?
8. What will experiencing the Spirit mean from these two passages?

3: The Spirit of adoption

We were made to live in families; to live in a relationship with parents who love us and care for us; to live in the security and comfort and assurance of that family. You can see that most clearly when it goes wrong. The distress and turmoil caused when we don't know the love of parents is immense. The sense of being lost when we don't feel we belong in a family is profound.

There was a heartbreaking TV documentary about children who were in care and hoping for adoption. They would spend some time with some possible 'parents to be'. They'd go on a day out together to see how they got on. Having been on such a day out, one child then drew pictures of himself with what he hoped would be his new 'Mum and Dad'. And so we see that desire for the experience of family.

That gives us a picture of the relationship between us and God. That relationship is often shown in the Bible as a child–parent relationship. When God first created people, that 'father–child' relationship was what he intended. We're told that Adam was created as 'the son of God' (Luke 3:38). But unfortunately this is a relationship that has broken down. Not because of bad parenting –

far from it! It's because we've decided to run away from home; we've decided to turn our back on God as our Father. So we too have become lost children – spiritually lost, this time.

Some people are very aware of being lost. They are aware that this relationship is missing and they are searching for it. They are homesick, if you like. Others, however, are completely oblivious to it; they have no sense of it at all. They may even be enjoying the freedom of it. But they are lost nonetheless. And despite their protestations to the contrary there are usually occasions when the confusion and awfulness of being lost descend on them as well.

What is very clear, though, is how God feels about this and what he wants to happen. He doesn't wait until we start searching for him; rather, he comes looking for us. It's our fault for turning away, but he wants to remedy it and bring us back into the family. And re-establishing that relationship involves the work of the Holy Spirit. God sends his Spirit into our lives so that we can know him and relate to him as our Father. That is a work of the Spirit that I think we haven't thought about as much as we should have done. And we neglect this at our peril. This goes to the very heart of our experience as Christians.

We are going to look at two passages, one from Galatians and one from Romans, both of which tie together the work of the Spirit with the fatherhood of God. Let's begin with this question:

Why did God send Jesus?

What did God want to achieve by Jesus' coming and living and dying and rising again? Well, it's there in Galatians 4:4–5:

> But when the time had fully come, God sent his Son, born of a woman, born under law, to redeem those under the law, that we might receive adoption as God's children.

The first answer is that God sent Jesus *to redeem us*. Redemption is the language of the slave market. If you went to a slave market and bought a slave (as you could easily do in Paul's day), and having bought him you set him free, you had just 'redeemed' him. It's paying a price to buy someone out of slavery. And that's what Jesus has done. He paid a price to set us free. We can see what that was back in Galatians 3:13: 'Christ redeemed us from the curse of the law by becoming a curse for us, for it is written: "Cursed is everyone who is hung on a tree." '

Our rebellion against God, our running away from home, means that we actually deserve what Paul calls this 'curse', which is God's punishment. But God sent Jesus to redeem us from that punishment, to free us from it. And Jesus did that, Paul says, by becoming a curse for us. That was the payment; he took the punishment, or the curse, in our place.

That is foundational to why God sent Jesus. And it is something we need to hold to and affirm clearly, because it is questioned more and more today. Many don't like the idea of 'punishment', and want to say that that wasn't really what was happening on the cross. I'd say from these verses, however, that that's exactly what was happening on the cross. But while this picture of redemption is foundational, we mustn't make the mistake of thinking that that is all that God wanted to achieve. Some people have emphasized this redemption – Jesus paying the price – and then stopped there. That is stopping short! God sent Jesus to achieve more than that. Back in 4:4–5 Paul says God sent Jesus to redeem us 'so that we might receive adoption as God's children'.

Literally he says it is 'so that we might receive the adoption'. The word Paul uses to speak of 'adoption as God's children' is a legal term that referred to the standing of the adopted male heir in Roman culture. These adopted sons had the same legal position as natural sons. So we become adopted children with the same position as the natural son. Clearly, there are many ways in which we are not like Jesus, but we become children of God as he is the Son of God, so much so that he becomes our 'brother' and we become joint heirs with him (Hebrews 2:11–12; Romans 8:17).

The Old Testament background to this idea of children and adoption is about God's relationship with Israel. When Israel is in slavery in Egypt God says, 'Israel is my firstborn son' (Exodus 4:22). Later, through the prophet Hosea, God looks back at that moment and says, 'When Israel was a child I loved him, and out of Egypt I called my son' (Hosea 11:1). We mentioned at the start of this chapter that God had created Adam and Eve to live in that 'father–children' relationship which was lost as we turned against God. So in these descriptions of Israel we see God restoring that relationship.

I know some people who are considering adoption. Why do they want to adopt a child? It's obvious, isn't it? It's for the relationship there will be with that child – so that they will know him or her as their child; so that that child will know them as parents. Deciding to adopt is about deciding to have a relationship. So God in the Old Testament was creating that loving relationship with his people Israel. And that is what he is doing now through Jesus.

So redemption is a stepping stone, if you like. It's a necessary stepping stone; you can't get across the river without it, but it's still a stepping stone to the other side. It's not God's ultimate purpose. Why did God send Jesus? So *we could be his children.*

God's ultimate aim explained here in Galatians 4 is to establish a new relationship. For that to happen, Jesus must first die in our place, and take the curse. But God isn't simply after our being 'free' rather than 'enslaved'; he wants us to be children. He sets us free so that we can go home with him. Similarly, we might emphasize that God sent Jesus to die to justify us – we are declared innocent because of his death in our place. That, too, is good and right, but also stops short of what God wants to achieve. God isn't simply after our being declared 'innocent' rather than 'guilty'. He wants us to be declared 'family'.

That's why God sent Jesus. He sent him because he wanted a

relationship with us. He sent him so that the adoption papers could be signed and we could go home with him and live with him as our Father.

You may be wondering at this stage: 'This is great, but I thought this was a book on the Holy Spirit.' Well, here it comes. We've seen why God sends Jesus; here's the next question:

Why does God send the Holy Spirit?

> Because you are his children, he sent the Spirit of his Son into our hearts, the Spirit who calls out, 'Abba, Father.' So you are no longer slaves, but God's children; and since you are his children, he has made you also heirs.
> (Galatians 4:6–7)

Did you see that there are two 'sendings' in these verses? In verse 4 God sent his Son, and then in verse 6 God sent the Spirit of his Son, the Holy Spirit. Why does he send him? God sends the Spirit so we can call him Father. Verse 6 says he sent the Spirit into our hearts, who calls out, 'Abba, Father'. The Spirit comes to make that relationship with God as Father real to us.

We see the same thing in the passage from Romans I want us to look at:

> You did not receive a spirit that makes you a slave again to fear, but you received the Spirit of adoption. And by him we cry, 'Abba, Father.' The Spirit himself testifies with our spirit that we are God's children.
> (Romans 8:15–16)

You see the similarity between the two passages? Once again we receive the Spirit, and it is linked to adoption, to sonship (it's the same word as back in Galatians 4). And once more the Spirit leads us to call God 'Abba, Father'. In the Galatians passage we're told it is the Spirit who cries out 'Abba, Father', but presumably it is through our lips. And in the Romans passage we get the fuller explanation that we say these words but we do so only 'by him', that is, by the Spirit. It is only by the work of the Spirit in our lives that we can call God Father and speak to him in prayer. This is why elsewhere Paul talks about praying 'in' or praying 'by' the Spirit (Ephesians 6:18). That's not a special form of prayer – that's the only way we can pray!

So these passages are showing us that a major work of the Spirit in our life is to call God, 'Abba, Father'. But of course we're talking here about much more than just what name we use. This is all about how we relate to God. God sends the Spirit so that we will *relate* to God as our Father.

Just think about a child being adopted today, an older child rather than an infant. To call these new parents 'Mum' and 'Dad' might not come naturally; it wouldn't just trip off the child's lips. Even if the child used those words quite quickly in this new relationship, he or she might still feel awkward and self-conscious. I would imagine that the day that child first said 'Dad' without being self-conscious or awkward about it would be a great day for both child and parents. It would be a great day because of what it would say about their relationship.

So in one sense these new parents aren't too bothered about the word used ('Mum' or 'Dad'); it's what the word signifies about the relationship that's important. They want a relationship of trust and closeness, intimacy and warmth. And the right word just signifies that.

It's the same here with us and God. God sends the Holy Spirit into our hearts and he leads us to call him '*Abba*, Father' because of what that tells us about the whole relationship. God sends the Holy Spirit so that we will relate to him as our Father just as Jesus did. That is why Paul specifically calls the Holy Spirit 'the Spirit of his Son' (verse 6). That is, the Spirit by whom Jesus related to God is now the Spirit who is in us. We can relate to God as Father, just as Jesus did, because we have the same Spirit.

Why say 'Abba'?

To drum this in a bit more we need to think about that word *Abba* for a moment. Paul gives us this Aramaic word 'Abba', and then gives a translation in Greek, 'Father'. But he includes the first word for a very good reason. That was the word that Jesus used when he prayed to God, his Father (see Mark 14:36). And Jesus was very unusual in using this word. The Jews of Jesus' day always prayed to God using a respectful term meaning 'Our Father'. It was quite formal, and Jesus clearly felt that that wasn't suitable for the sort of relationship he had with God.

There was another word he could have used which was a more familiar, personal word, which meant something like 'my Father'. The Jews wouldn't have dared use that of God, but it seems that for Jesus that, too, wasn't appropriate. It didn't capture the openness, the freedom, the intimacy, that he had with his Father. And so he used the word *Abba*. It was a very domestic word; you'd only hear it in close family. It's a bit like the way we use 'Daddy' – not that it was simply the word of young children, but it was the word of close family. That word captured something of the warmth and closeness of Jesus' relationship with his Father.

So do you see why Paul deliberately includes that word here? He's saying that we're given the Spirit so that we can say the same thing that Jesus did; so that we can relate to God in the same way that Jesus did. We approach God our Father just as Jesus did. Our position is the same, after all. He is the son by right, whereas we are children by adoption – but it's the same position. And so we use the same word. The New Testament scholar Gordon Fee explains it like this: 'The Spirit has taken us far beyond mere conformity to religious obligations. God himself, in the person of his Spirit, has come to indwell us; and he has sealed that relationship by giving to us the language of his Son, the language of personal relationship.'

Make the relationship real

Charles Spurgeon was a famous minister in London in the nineteenth century. Some people had noticed the way he prayed in church services and had said it was too familiar; they felt it really wasn't appropriate that he should speak like that with God. He replied in the following way: 'I see it is alleged as a very grave charge against me that I speak as if I were familiar with God. But I know I am his child and with whom should a child be familiar but with his father?' Exactly!

God doesn't want us to lose our sense of awe or reverence for him, but he does want us to call him 'Father'; that's why he sent his Spirit. To put it another way, God sent the Spirit to *make our relationship real*. You see, the relationship could be real in the sense that the papers were signed; we could be legally adopted. But we all know there's a world of difference between a legal reality and a relational reality. And without the Spirit there would be no means of our truly relating to God as Father. Without the Spirit God would be remote and distant and we would be fearful and anxious in our relationship with him.

But this is exactly what God wants to counter. Romans 8:15 says, 'The Spirit you received does not make you slaves, so that you live in fear again; rather, the Spirit you received brought about your adoption to sonship.' That is, the Spirit leads you to relate to God as a Father whom you can trust, rather than a God you are only fearful of.

Paul puts the same thing a different way in verse 16: 'The Spirit himself testifies with our spirit that we are God's children.' I don't think he's talking about something new in this verse. He's just said that the Spirit gives us the confidence to call God 'Father', to relate to him that way. And here he is simply saying that that experience reassures us that we really are God's children. So the testimony of the Spirit that we are God's children is simply our experience of being able to call God '*Abba*, Father', and relate to him as such.

So we must again realize that this isn't simply an issue of belief. This isn't something you put on a statement of faith: 'We believe that by the Spirit we know God as Father.' It is, of course, a truth we believe, but more than that it is a relationship we experience.

The experience of God as Father

Now some people ask, 'What do I experience, exactly?', or say, 'I've not had much of an experience', or 'Other people seem to have more of an experience than me.' How shall we respond? Well, first, we must make it clear what sort of experience we're talking about here.

I think of my children. As far as I know they don't go through life *feeling* that I am their father. In fact, I'm not sure what a 'feeling that I am father' would feel like! Rather, what they do is they go through life *relating* to me as their father. They ask me for things, they talk to me, they run to me when they're hurt, they respond in trust when I makes promises (usually, anyway!).

This is the stuff of experiencing me as father. It's the experience of a relationship. And that's the sort of experience we're talking about with God. I don't think the Spirit brings a feeling that God simply is Father; he brings us to relate to God as Father. So we have confidence in him, so we know his love, we know his acceptance, we trust him, we ask him for help, we say sorry to him, we run to him for his comfort. This isn't something you sit and feel; it's a relationship you live in.

Other verses in the New Testament give us insight into this. For example, Romans 5:5 speaks of our knowing God's love, and says we know it through the work of the Holy Spirit: 'God has poured out his love into our hearts by the Holy Spirit, whom he has given us.' Romans 15:13 talks about how it's the work of the Holy Spirit that will bring us joy and peace and hope: 'May the God of hope fill you with all joy and peace as you trust in him, so that you may overflow with hope by the power of the Holy Spirit.' Ephesians 2:18 tells us how our relationship with God and access to him depends on the work of the Spirit as well as of Jesus: 'For through him [Jesus] we both have access to the Father by one Spirit.'

So, first, we need to be clear on what sort of experience we're talking about: it's the experience of a relationship. And I take it that all Christians know the experience of relating to God in this way.

Secondly, there will be variation in what each person feels at different times. Sometimes we will feel some of those things – say, my acceptance with God – with much greater intensity than at other times. Let me give you an example. John Wesley (an eighteenth-century minister) is well known for describing his experience when listening to an explanation of the gospel. He said, 'I felt my heart strangely warmed.' And he went on to speak about being assured of forgiveness and so on.

But he was probably converted before that event. That event was a moment of realization when God brought these things home to him. And that heart-warming feeling didn't last. He didn't then walk around on a spiritual high from that point onwards. Our experience of God will vary over time. For me there are times when God feels very close. I find that especially when I reflect with others in singing praise to God. That's not uncommon because singing is an emotive activity which can raise our emotional temperature. At other times I feel very little. But I still relate to God as my Father; I speak to him, turn to him, trust him. So it will vary for each of us over time.

And, lastly, we also need to notice that this experience of God will vary between us. Some people would say they've never had a heart-warming experience at all, but that doesn't mean they don't relate to God as Father. If that's you, I'd like to reassure you of that. I think a lot of this depends on our personalities; some of us have emotional ranges that go from the heights to the depths. Others of us are more emotionally limited. Or you could say more emotionally stable, depending on how you want to look at it. I don't think God changes us so that we all have identical personalities and identical feelings. He is worried only that we all have a *real* relationship with him.

And so I also want to say that we need to be careful in the way we each speak of our experience of God. It is very easy for some who either are more expressive or have had a greater intensity of experience (or both) to speak in such a way that others are made to feel that they don't really know God at all. That is both untrue and unhelpful, and we need to be careful with each other. What we should do, of course, is pray to God that by his Spirit we would all grow in our relationship with him. Not necessarily grow in our depths of feeling or emotion, but grow in the reality of that relationship.

Not lost any more

Remember where we started? We are lost – separated from God because we've turned away from him. The most foundational relationship we can and should have in life is missing. But God has sent his Son to redeem us so that we can become sons; and he's sent the Spirit of his Son so that we will call him Father. So if we trust in Christ, we're not lost children any more. That defining relationship has been re-established.

Doesn't that encourage you, when you get up in the morning, to talk to your Father in heaven? Doesn't that encourage you, when you hit trouble or anxiety this week, to turn to your Father? Doesn't that encourage you to grow to know your Father, to hear him speaking to you through his Word? Doesn't that encourage you to live life looking to your Father in all you do? Doesn't that encourage you, because that relationship is real?

study 3

Galatians 4:4–7; Romans 8:15–17

Read Galatians 4:4–7

1. Why does Paul say God sent Jesus? What is his ultimate aim?
2. Having sent his Son, why does God then send the Spirit of his Son?
3. What is the significance of saying that the Spirit calls out 'Abba, Father'?
4. What does being 'heirs' mean for how we should view the future?

Read Romans 8:15–17

5. What are the similarities to and differences from the passage in Galatians?
6. Paul suggests that the work of the Spirit is the opposite of being a slave to fear. Why is this the case?
7. How does the Spirit reassure us of our adoption?
8. What does experiencing the Spirit mean from these two passages?

1 Corinthians 2:6-16

H. G. Wells wrote a story called *The Country of the Blind*. It's about a remote valley that is cut off from the rest of the world. And in this valley, owing to a genetic disorder, everyone is blind from birth. It's been that way for generations. To this community blindness is normal; they simply don't know what it is to be able to see. And one day a mountaineer stumbles into this valley. The story is then about the entrance of this sighted person into the country of the blind.

You can imagine how they all respond. They think *he's* abnormal. In fact, they consider him deranged. He has these fanciful ideas about what he calls 'vision' and 'seeing'. He has ludicrous notions about a part of his body he calls his 'eyes'. To them the man was clearly sick! They discuss the matter among themselves and decide they have a solution, a way they can 'cure' him. They will put out these eyes he talks about, and then he'll be normal, like the rest of them.

It's a powerful picture of one group not being able to understand another, a picture in which something is so alien to people's experience that they cannot understand it. Not only can they not understand it; they react by ridiculing it and trying to eliminate it.

That's the sort of picture Paul is describing in this passage about the work of the Holy Spirit.

The blindness of the world

We do, however, speak a message of wisdom among the mature, but not the wisdom of this age or of the rulers of this age, who are coming to nothing. No, we speak of God's secret wisdom, a wisdom that has been hidden and that God destined for our glory before time began. None of the rulers of this age understood it, for if they had, they would not have crucified the Lord of glory.
(1 Corinthians 2:6–8)

One of the things going on in the city of Corinth was that the church had become fascinated with 'wisdom'. At least, they were fascinated by what the world regarded as wisdom. They were probably caught up with the fine-sounding rhetoric of public speakers, so that they were concerned only about how impressive something sounded and how clever it appeared. They loved speakers with the gift of the gab.

Paul has been discussing this in the opening chapter of his letter. He picks up on it again in the verses above and basically says, 'We do speak a wise message, but it's not the wisdom of this world; it's not the wisdom of the rulers of this world.' He's saying his wisdom operates on a different basis from that of the world's opinion-makers, the movers and shakers, the ones who sounded so clever. If you look back to chapter 1 and verse 20, you'll see he listed these people there: the wise man, the scholar, and the philosopher of this age.

Today, for some of us, I guess we're talking about the scientist, the psychologist, the sociologist, or the cultural pundit who writes the editorials. For others of us it's the film star, the pop idol, the fashion guru, the sports personality. It's the person we look to to say what's what, the person who sways our thinking, the person who influences our opinions. They are the people we and our culture follow.

But Paul's point is this: the wisdom of this world is blind, and the rulers of this world are only the blind leading the blind. In verse 7 Paul says that their wisdom and insight cannot understand God or his plan: 'we speak of God's secret wisdom . . . None of the rulers of this age understood it.'

He says this wisdom of God's has been hidden and these rulers can't discover it. They don't understand it. And I can prove it to you, he says. The proof is in how they responded to Jesus. Verse 8 says that if they had understood it, they wouldn't have crucified Jesus. That just goes to show how far short they fall of understanding God and his plans – they killed his Son; they didn't recognize the Lord of glory. That reaction shows how blind they are.

In verse 9, Paul goes on to quote from Isaiah 64:4 about God's plans:

'No eye has seen,
　no ear has heard,
no mind has conceived
　what God has prepared for those who love him.'

No-one is able to work out what God has in store or what God's plans are. No eye can *see* it; no matter what telescope or microscope is used, it's invisible to them. No ear can *hear* it; whatever listening device you use, it is inaudible. No mind can *conceive* of it; no matter which philosophers you ask, no matter what surveys you perform, this remains inconceivable to the rulers of this age. They might sound clever, they might be very intelligent, they might be right about all sorts of stuff, but when it comes to God and his plans, they've got no idea. The world is blind and cannot understand God or his plans.

A friend of mine once told me about a trip he went on, to a huge cavern in a mountainside in South Africa. This cavern was absolutely vast; apparently it was the size of a cathedral inside. But as the tour group walked in, the guide showed them the way with just a torch. There was enough light for them to see the floor where they were walking and the odd spot on the wall. But if the guide shone his torch up into the air the light just faded into blackness. So they knew they were in some big area, but they couldn't see their surroundings at all – until the guide flicked on some huge neon lights that lit up the whole place and everyone gasped.

The wisdom of our world is a bit like walking round with a torch. We can see a few bits and pieces here and there, and then, in our arrogance, we easily declare we know everything about everything, whereas in reality we're peering into the darkness. In fact, because we can see only a few bits and pieces around us we can't even place them properly in the grand scheme of things. What we need is for God to turn the lights on. Or, rather, we need him to open our eyes. After all, the problem isn't that God has left us in the dark – the problem is that we're blind to him.

I heard a series of talks on the radio called 'The Emerging Mind'. It was about understanding the human brain. And there was some fascinating stuff in these lectures; it was very impressive, and clearly there was a remarkable person behind this research who'd made some great discoveries. One of the lectures touched on whether we had a soul and on our consciousness of God.

In the question time someone asked the lecturer, 'Do you believe in God?'

He replied, 'If you mean some impersonal force out there somewhere, maybe. But if you mean an old guy who's watching me and will punish me, no.'

The questioner asked, 'Is that because of science?'

To which he replied, 'It's partly common sense.'

And the audience laughed.

I thought that that was a remarkable moment, because he admitted that his science, brilliant as it was, couldn't answer the question. And yet he clearly thought he knew the answer, and so mocked the idea of the Christian God – or at least a caricature of it. That is the arrogance of the wisdom of this age, which is blind to God.

And, as we mentioned above, this world in its blindness opposes God. The brightest and best of the Jewish government and the Roman Empire were an example of this wisdom of the world when they crucified Jesus, the Lord of glory. In doing so, they showed their true colours. That's the bottom line on this wisdom: it might say it's searching for the truth; it might even say it's searching for God. But when God appears in the flesh, it murders him. And that, says Paul, is where the blindness of this world takes you, because fundamentally this world is anti-truth and anti-God. We like being in charge ourselves too much, you see.

And so you can be sure that the opinion-makers of today (unless they're Christians, of course), whether from science or the media or wherever, will push on us wisdom that opposes God. And so of all the worldviews out there, of all the philosophies of life, we shouldn't be surprised if the Christian gospel is the most rejected and despised. This is why.

So when you hear that sort of stuff, don't be threatened by it, don't be intimidated. We can be so easily cowed because we're made to feel we're the odd ones out, we're the ones who need help, just like the mountaineer in the valley. Except that he was the one who had sight. Our society might sound so very clever, but it is actually blind.

All of this raises a question: if we are all naturally blind like this, if we can't discover God for ourselves, how will we ever know him?

The Spirit who opens our eyes

Paul said in verses 6–7 that he is speaking a message of wisdom, the message of God's secret wisdom, which has been hidden. How can he speak of this thing that he has just said is invisible, inaudible and inconceivable? The last line of verse 10 tells us: 'God has revealed it to us by his Spirit.'

And the rest of the passage explores that idea. He has two main points to make. First, *the Spirit knows God*.

> The Spirit searches all things, even the deep things of God.
> For who knows the thoughts of another human being except
> that person's own spirit within? In the same way no-one
> knows the thoughts of God except the Spirit of God.
> (Verses 10–11)

If I were standing in front of you right now, could you tell me what I was thinking? No, my thoughts are hidden from you: you can't see them, you can't hear them and you can't guess them. But my spirit knows what I'm thinking. It's the same with God, says Paul: no-one knows the thoughts of God, the things of God, except the Spirit of God. In fact, he searches them out; he's like a deep-sea diver plumbing the depths of God's thoughts.

Secondly, not only does the Spirit know God, the Spirit reveals God. See how Paul goes on in verse 12: 'We have not received the spirit of the world but the Spirit who is from God, that we may understand what God has freely given us.'

The spirit of the world is a reference back to the wisdom of this age, the thinking of this world, which is so blind. We haven't received that spirit, says Paul; we've received God's own Spirit, the one who knows him and his thoughts. He's given us the Holy Spirit so that we can understand what God has done in Jesus. In other words, God has turned the lights on.

Clearly, having the Spirit doesn't mean we know everything God knows – we don't become omniscient, knowing every-thing possible. But we can know truly. We can have our eyes opened so that we can see beyond what was previously possible – those things that God has prepared for those who love him – his wonderful plans of salvation – which were previously invisible, inaudible and inconceivable to us (verse 9). We can now know these things. God mercifully reveals them to us by his Spirit. He's given us the Spirit so that we may 'understand what God has freely given us'.

This is both humbling and wonderfully encouraging. It's humbling because we are being told we need the Holy Spirit in us even to understand what God has done in Jesus. Without that work of the Spirit we will remain blind. But it's wonderfully encouraging, because God *wants* us to understand. He wants us to know the truth of all he's done and will do through Jesus, and that's why he gives us his Spirit – so that we can understand what he has freely given us.

A two-stage process

Now we need to understand that this process of revelation can be divided into two parts. See what Paul says in verse 13: 'This is what we speak, not in words taught us by human wisdom but in words taught by the Spirit, expressing spiritual truths in spiritual words.'

The first people to receive the Spirit and to understand what God has done were Paul and the other apostles. And so Paul can say in verse 13 that the message *we're* speaking is not a message taught by human wisdom; rather, it's a message taught by the Spirit. Paul and others spoke these spiritual truths they'd been given and they wrote those truths down in their letters. We see another reference to this in Ephesians 3, where Paul talks about the mystery of Christ, 'which was not made known to people in other generations as it has now been revealed by the Spirit to God's holy apostles and prophets' (verse 5).

We can digress a little here and look at another verse that speaks about how God guided people to speak and to write his words to others. Peter says the following in 2 Peter 1:20–21: 'Above all, you must understand that no prophecy of Scripture came about by the prophet's own interpretation. For prophecy never had its origin in the human will, but prophets, though human, spoke from God as they were carried along by the Holy Spirit.'

The picture is that of a boat with a sail being blown along by the wind. The Holy Spirit blew people along so that they understood and said what God wanted them to. We saw the same thing in a previous chapter, on the Holy Spirit and Jesus, where Jesus promised to send his apostles the Holy Spirit to remind them and teach them. And, similarly, Paul can say he speaks words of spiritual truth taught by the Spirit.

He can say that; we *can't*. This is the process of revelation to inspire people so that they speak and write God's truth. That process has now happened and it isn't repeated. We, then, are like these Corinthians, those who hear these words of truth from someone like Paul, or from someone who learns it from Paul and tells it to us. In other words, we don't all get a private revelation of what God has done. If we did, then there'd be no need to tell anyone the good news about Jesus. There'd be no need ever to teach anyone more about Jesus from the Bible.

But – and it's a big 'but' – we then need that same work of the Spirit in our hearts and minds in order to understand these words. The Spirit has to keep working, every time the message is passed on, to open blind eyes. See how Paul puts it in 1 Corinthians 2:14–15:

> The person without the Spirit does not accept the things that come from the Spirit of God, but considers them foolishness, and cannot understand them because they are spiritually discerned. The person with the Spirit makes judgments about all things, but such a person is not subject to merely human judgments.

If you don't have the Spirit working to open your eyes, you can't discern this message. You can hear these words of truth, but they are foolishness to you; you think it's all rubbish. But the spiritual person – that is, the person with the Spirit – can discern the message. This person can understand.

When Paul says that this person is not subject to anyone else's judgment, I think he means that other people won't understand this spiritual sight this person has. He or she isn't subject to their discernment, because his or her eyes have been opened and theirs haven't. That's why Paul quotes again from Isaiah 40:13:

> 'For who has known the mind of the Lord
>   so as to instruct him?'

But we have the mind of Christ.

We're back to where we started. No-one can know the mind of God – the world is blind – but we have been given the mind of Christ so that we can understand. We are like the sighted man in the valley of the blind, and so we aren't subject to their evaluation of our sight.

Can you see the letter?

To test for colour blindness, opticians use a special chart. It has numbers within a pattern of dots. So, for example, the background dots are coloured green and the dots making up the letter within them are coloured red. If you're colour-blind you can't see the difference between the two colours and so you can't see the letter.

When we hear the message of the gospel, we are naturally colour-blind to it – we can't understand it; it is foolishness to us. In the analogy, we can't see the letter in the dots. And so we need the Spirit to cure our colour blindness, so that we can discern the letter. And if we don't have the Spirit we can't see it.

In *The Country of the Blind*, they thought not seeing was normal, and so the bloke who spoke of sight was mad; he spoke foolishness, they thought. He, of course, could imagine what it would be like not to see; he could put himself in their shoes. But they couldn't get into his. They couldn't understand what he was speaking about, unless someone restored their sight.

That is what Paul is saying the world is like. We are all naturally blind. But God has revealed himself and his truth. He has opened people's eyes to see. And they then speak to others and tell them of this truth. And God works again, giving sight; but if he doesn't, it remains foolishness.

Spiritual sight and evangelism

The first implication is for our evangelism. If the Spirit's role is to open people's eyes, then our job is to be faithful in telling people the gospel, not in making them understand it. I don't mean we shouldn't explain and try to persuade and so on; we certainly should do that. What I mean is that we can't get inside people to make them see the truth of the gospel, but the Spirit can. He will use us and our explanations, but we must trust him to bring the light to shine – this is the same point that we saw in the chapter on the Spirit and Jesus.

So Paul rejoices over the Thessalonians' conversion, as he says this: 'For we know, brothers and sisters loved by God, that he has chosen you, because our gospel came to you not simply with words but also with power, with the Holy Spirit and with deep conviction' (1 Thessalonians 1:4–5).

This also explains our experience in evangelism. One day, and with one person, you can explain the gospel as clearly as crystal, and the person just doesn't seem to get it. In fact, he or she laughs at you and thinks you're weird for talking about such stuff. But tell the gospel to a different person on the same day, or the same person on a different day, and the person might suddenly say, 'I understand.' That gives me great confidence in telling people the gospel. I just have to explain; God is doing his work of opening their eyes by his Spirit.

Spiritual sight and our culture

Secondly, this has huge implications for living in our culture. We've spoken about the 'rulers of our age', the opinion-makers.

The main people we're talking about are those we hear in the media, be it TV, radio, magazine, newspaper, or the Web. We will hear them say that Bible-believing Christians are old-fashioned and narrow-minded idiots who need to get into the twenty-first century. Perhaps they'll even call us fundamentalists. We so easily feel the barb of their words and allow them to cow us into silence and embarrassment about the gospel. This passage teaches us that we must realize that they are blind to God's truth. They may sound clever but actually they speak foolishness. And so we must not let ourselves be intimidated.

Imagine how that guy in the valley of the blind would have been made to feel. They'd have called him stupid, an idiot and so on. They would have mocked his ridiculous idea of 'seeing'. But he was the one with true sight! He'd have had to keep on reminding himself, 'I'm not the blind one here.' We must do the same. We must remind ourselves that the work of the Spirit has given us sight. And so we should have confidence in the face of our culture and its supposed wisdom.

We must note, though, that this truth should result in confidence but not in pride. It is quite possible for Christians to become rather condescending and superior to those around them – 'They haven't been enlightened like we have; poor things, they don't understand.' As we've seen from this passage, such comments do, of course, carry some truth. But it is the tone and manner of them that are wrong. We have been given new spiritual sight and so have been 'enlightened', but only as a gift of God's grace. It is something to be grateful for, not to take pride in.

Spiritual sight and reading the Bible

The last area I want us to think about is in reading the Bible generally. This passage in 1 Corinthians focuses on how we come to understand the gospel in the first place, but the way God reveals himself doesn't suddenly change once we become Christians. We continually need God to reveal himself to us more and more by his Spirit through his Word.

So, for example, Paul says in Ephesians 1:17: 'I keep asking that the God of our Lord Jesus Christ, the glorious Father, may give you the Spirit of wisdom and revelation, so that you may know him better.' Here's another prayer, from Psalm 119:18: 'Open my eyes that I may see wonderful things in your law.' And here's some advice from Paul to Timothy in 2 Timothy 2:7: 'Reflect on what I am saying, for the Lord will give you insight into all this.'

We should be asking God to reveal himself to us by his Spirit as we read his Word. We remain dependent on him. We will always tend to blindness and we continually need him to shine his light and open our eyes so that we know him better.

I sometimes speak to people who seem to have reached a plateau in their Christian life. They look back at times of growth, but that all seems in the past; right now they're not really going anywhere. There can be lots of reasons for that, but here's a key one: stopping praying that God will help us to know him better; stopping asking God to open our eyes so that we see wonderful things; stopping reflecting on Scripture, asking God to give us insight.

Notice, from that last verse quoted, that we remain active in this process. The fact that God is the one opening our eyes and revealing himself doesn't mean we just lie back and wait for him to do it. Paul tells Timothy to 'reflect', that is, to think things over and reason them out. But as he does the reflecting God will give him insight. There's a wonderful balance there that I think we often miss. If we reason something by ourselves and come to a new understanding, we tend to say, 'I've understood it; I've worked it out', not 'God granted me insight'.

But it's just the same as when we came to believe the gospel. When you believed the gospel, it was not because you were clever enough to decide to believe it, so that you could say to yourself 'Well done, me!' You understood it only because God opened your eyes, and so you say, 'Thank you, God.'

We must think hard about the Bible and reflect on it. We must discuss it together, listen to sermons, read books. We must continue to use our minds, because the normal processes of understanding and comprehension aren't suspended when it comes to understanding God. But we do it all humbly dependent on God, confidently trusting that he will open our eyes and grant us insight.

So be humble, but also be confident that you can understand. I'm not saying that everything is easy to understand, because it's not. And I'm not saying that teachers in the church aren't useful to us, because they are. And I'm not saying that any sort of theological training isn't helpful to us in reading the Bible, because it is. But I am saying you can grow to know God better as you read his Word and the Spirit opens your eyes.

Do you believe it?

Have you heard of William Tyndale? He lived in the sixteenth century. He believed that ordinary Christians with God's Spirit in their heart could understand the Bible. And so he believed that ordinary Christians should have a Bible in their hands in their language and that they should be encouraged to read it. He believed it so much that he translated the Bible into English. (At the time, the only Bibles around were in Latin, which most people couldn't read.) He believed it so much that he carried on translating even when his life was threatened. In fact, he believed it so much that he was burnt at the stake because of it.

William Tyndale was confident that people like you and me could understand what God has given us because his Spirit reveals it to us. Can I ask you if you believe that? If you do, you don't have to show it by translating the Bible for others and risking being burnt alive. You'll show it by reading the Bible yourself, confident that God will speak by his Spirit.

study 4

1 Corinthians 2:6–16

1. The message of the gospel is a message of wisdom, but not the wisdom of the world (verse 6). What does this mean?
2. What does Paul say about people being able to discover God's wisdom by themselves? How does this mean we should view our human reasoning?
3. How does he say we have come to know God's wisdom?
4. What express reason does Paul give for God sending his Spirit (verse 12)? What does this mean in practice?
5. How does this work of the Spirit influence the way Paul views his own explanations of the gospel (verse 13)?
6. How does this work of the Spirit explain different reactions to hearing the gospel (verses 14–15)?
7. How does this mean we should think about our own understanding of spiritual things? What attitude should we have about how much we know?
8. How does this mean we should approach 'learning' about God?
9. What does experiencing the Spirit mean from this passage?

Galatians 5:16–26

I'm sure you know the story of Dr Jekyll and Mr Hyde by Robert Louis Stevenson. Dr Jekyll is a respectable London doctor who discovers a potion. Whenever he takes it, it turns him into the despicable Mr Hyde. And in the form of Mr Hyde he performs all sorts of horrible deeds.

But although Dr Jekyll is ashamed of what he does as Mr Hyde, he's addicted to becoming this alter ego. He tries to resist occasionally, but he always ends up giving in and taking the potion once again. In fact, it gets worse and worse and this evil side of his personality starts to dominate him. In the end he finds he has actually become Mr Hyde and cannot return to being Dr Jekyll. And he commits suicide.

It is, of course, much more than simply a good horror story. It's a profound comment on the state of humanity and our struggle with evil within us. After all, it's not that the horrible person of Mr Hyde is someone different from Dr Jekyll. Jekyll himself knows that Mr Hyde is actually a distillation of part of himself. In fact, at one point in explicitly commenting about Mr Hyde he admits, 'This too is myself.'

Stevenson is saying that, no matter how pleasant and respectable people may appear, there is a leaning towards evil within them. We each have this side to us, which tempts us and draws us. And in the final analysis, for Stevenson at least, we are not able to resist it or control it. Of course, the story of Jekyll and Hyde paints that picture for us in a pretty over-the-top sort of way; it's like a caricatured picture. But, as with most good caricatures, I expect we all recognize ourselves.

An embarrassing truth

In many ways Stevenson has captured a biblical truth about the nature of humanity. Ever since we humans turned against God in the 'fall' (see Genesis 3), we have had this bent towards evil. The biblical writers are unembarrassed about it. In fact, Jesus is unembarrassed about it. Do you remember his comment about the state of our hearts?

> 'What comes out of you is what makes you "unclean". For from within, out of your hearts, come evil thoughts, sexual immorality, theft, murder, adultery, greed, malice, deceit, lewdness, envy, slander, arrogance and folly. All these evils come from inside and make you "unclean".'
> (Mark 7:20–23)

Where does Jesus think that 'evil' comes from? Is it from our backgrounds, our upbringing, or our genes? No, Jesus is very clear that the source of evil is to be located in our hearts. When we see some of the horrible things we can think, do and be, we can't say to ourselves, 'That wasn't really me.' Rather, with Dr Jekyll, we have to look our evil side in the face and say, 'This too is myself.'

In fact, we have to go further. It's not just that we have an evil 'side' to ourselves. Rather, as Jesus mentions in passing, we *are* evil (Matthew 7:11). It's a pretty absolute statement, isn't it? But that is the biblical picture. We certainly feel the stab of conscience and we are certainly capable of doing better and worse things. But in relation to God we are evil. Paul puts it like this in his letter to the Romans (8:7–8): 'The sinful mind is hostile to God. It does not submit to God's law, nor can it do so. Those controlled by the sinful nature cannot please God.'

When Paul talks about 'those controlled by the sinful nature' there, he is referring to people whose whole existence is determined by their sinful nature. More literally, it is those who are 'of the flesh' – 'the flesh' is Paul's word for our old nature which is rebellious against God. And he's describing life when that was in charge, when that determined who we were.

And do you see what an awful description it is? Those living in the sinful nature are hostile to God, he says. They fight against God; they are unable to obey him or please him. Now we may immediately think to ourselves, 'But I know lots of nice non-Christians, who do really good things. Surely they please God, at least occasionally?' Well, they may do things that are objectively 'good', and in that sense God approves of it. But do they please him by doing it? No, not at all; they cannot, because at the heart of their being they are still fighting him.

Here's an illustration. You can be rebellious against the government of the country and so completely disregard the law. So you might break the speed limit, which would show that rebellion. Alternatively, you might decide to drive within the speed limit, because you choose to do so. But you may be no less rebellious – you've still chosen what speed to drive at yourself, with no regard for what the government says. The action is in one sense 'better' in the second case, but the attitude is identical. So people may do 'good' things, but they do them because they choose to do so, and their attitude to God remains hostile, and they do not please him.

That's where the story of Jekyll and Hyde is misleading. You might think there was a chance that Jekyll's better side might win the day. But actually, according to the Bible, there is no 'better side'; there is only the sinful nature. We might feel the prick of our conscience or the pressure of other people's expectations, and in that sense we may *feel* a fight within us. But in reality there is no fight; we are controlled by the sinful nature. The story of Jekyll and Hyde really shows only how we may try to present ourselves to other people as pleasant or respectable, or how we try to think about ourselves. But we are evil; we cannot please God. I'm sorry to say that the Bible has this very bleak picture of our moral state. However, I'm glad to say that the pessimism ends when God works in us by his Spirit.

The fight begins

As we've seen in previous chapters, when we become Christians God re-creates us by his Spirit. We are born again and come alive in a new way. God's Spirit now lives in us. And that opens up the possibility of now living a life that can please God, a life that can submit to his law and obey him.

Previously we could not but sin; our sinful nature dominated all that we did. Now we have the possibility of not sinning. And that possibility is there only because of this re-creation by the Spirit. But we are not completely remade. Rather, the sinful nature is still there – it won't be remade until we're given new bodies. And so there is now going to be a fight. The fight is between the Spirit on one side and the sinful nature on the other.

We can see Paul describing it in Galatians 5:16–17:

So I say, live by the Spirit, and you will not gratify the desires of the sinful nature. For the sinful nature desires what is contrary to the Spirit, and the Spirit what is contrary to the sinful nature. They are in conflict with each other, so that you do not do what you want.

You see the conflict between the two? They desire contrary things; they want to pull us in opposite directions; they are opposed to each other. Paul goes on to describe the contrary effects these two will have on our life. Let's look at them in turn and then we'll come back to the idea of this fight.

The pull of the sinful nature

This is the pull towards evil we've mentioned already, which leads us to desire what is wrong. Paul describes it in Galatians 5:19–21:

> The acts of the sinful nature are obvious: sexual immorality, impurity and debauchery; idolatry and witchcraft; hatred, discord, jealousy, fits of rage, selfish ambition, dissensions, factions and envy; drunkenness, orgies, and the like. I warn you, as I did before, that those who live like this will not inherit the kingdom of God.

Let's make a few observations about this list. Firstly, it isn't exhaustive. When Paul says 'and the like' (verse 21), he means that he could go on: this isn't all of them; these are just the first ones to come to mind. But there's enough to give you the general idea.

Secondly, notice that these evil actions cover all sorts of areas of life. They include sexuality, religion, relationships and personal attitudes. In other words, the sinful nature can and does show itself in any and every area of life.

Thirdly, we should see that this list ranges from what we might tend to think of as really bad, all the way to what we might consider pretty minor. Some of us will read the bits about witchcraft, orgies or debauchery and say, 'Well, I'm not perfect, but at least I haven't done that.' But read on. There's also being jealous, or falling out with people. We quite like to grade sins, but Paul doesn't bother – they are all acts of the sinful nature. They all come from the same place.

It's just possible, however, that you have done what we think of as the really bad stuff and may feel awful about it. You may feel that everyone else is a decent sort of person and you are the odd one out. Well, others may not have done some of the things you have, but they have a sinful nature too. It may have shown itself in different ways, but it is no less real. This list describes us all and brings us all to the same level. There should be no reason to feel worse than others or better than others.

Lastly, notice that you can produce these acts of the sinful nature and still look very respectable. For example, if you are jealous and hate people, that can show itself in being openly bitter and condemning of others. Or you might keep it all simmering below the surface. Likewise, sexual immorality might mean you sleep around all the time and people know it, or it might all be in your head and no-one else is any the wiser.

In New York there was once a strike by the bin men and consequently people couldn't get rid of their rubbish. One bright spark hit on a solution to dispose of their rubbish. He collected lots of boxes from Macy's, an upmarket department store. He put his rubbish in one of these posh Macy's boxes and left it outside his apartment. Every time he did it, it was then stolen that night – presumably by someone thinking there was something valuable inside this smart box.

That is how we can be morally. We can look great on the outside, and can be very presentable – so much so, in fact, that people would think we are pretty good on the inside. But actually we're not. As I said, you can live out these acts of the sinful nature and show it, or you can look quite moral.

This, then, is what Stevenson called Mr Hyde. At one point in the story Dr Jekyll reflects on becoming Mr Hyde and says that he was conscious of no repugnance, but rather there was the 'leap of welcome'. He actually wanted to be like this. So with us: our sinful nature pulled us to live like this and to want to live like this. There may have been the odd pang of conscience, but we were only living out what we were. Once remade by the Spirit, we are now different inside and so can live differently. But the pull of the sinful nature to all this sort of stuff will still be there, and we will still feel it.

The pull of the Spirit

Just as the sinful nature led to those acts of evil, the Holy Spirit leads us to produce his good actions, or his 'fruit'. See Galatians 5:22–23:

> But the fruit of the Spirit is love, joy, peace, patience, kindness, goodness, faithfulness, gentleness and self-control. Against such things there is no law.

Let's make a few comments on this list of fruit, as we did above. Firstly, in this list Paul doesn't finish by saying 'and the like', as he did with the previous list, but the idea is probably the same. He could have easily added a couple more. Where, for example, are the Christian characteristics of 'forgiveness', or 'humility', or 'generosity'? This is a good representative list, but it's not exhaustive.

Secondly, notice that these are the 'fruit' (singular) of the Spirit, not the 'fruits' (plural). That is, Paul thinks of these characteristics as like one multifaceted fruit. So we can't look down the list and say, 'Well I'm OK on patience, and peace, but it's a shame about love.' This isn't a case of picking your best three scores. There is a unity about these. While we will, of course, be more developed on some than others, they are supposed to grow together.

Notice, thirdly, that this is not a list of rules. It's not about drawing lines between right and wrong, and saying that the Spirit leads you not to cross the line. It's not about lines you cross; this is all about attitudes you develop and express. This isn't a rulebook; it's a character description. And what God wants is for us to develop these godly characters. He wants us to become kind, to become self-controlled, and so on. He wants us to show this fruit so that if you looked at how I behaved in my relationships, or approached my work, or treated my family, or went about my hobbies, or played my sports, or whatever else I did, these qualities would be true of me. Whatever slice of my life you took, you would see these as character traits running through me.

This is linked with the comments Paul makes in this passage

about law. Back in verse 18 he said, 'But if you are led by the Spirit, you are not under law.' His argument with false teachers in Galatia was about the role of the Old Testament law in Christian living. They wanted to push it on people and tell them they had to live by it to grow as Christians or perhaps even to stay Christians. But Paul sees that, for Christians, the dynamic of living is not external, a rule that coerces us, but rather internal, a Spirit that leads us.

Lastly, we need to see that this means that the fruit keeps on growing and growing. I think this is why Paul picks the metaphor of fruit. You can never say, 'I've done it; tick the box.' If it was a list of rules, you could do that, if you ever obeyed them all. But this is a character that we keep on growing in. This fruit continues to develop and we can never say, 'We're done.'

This illustration is well known but it bears repeating. Think of some person whose talents you admire. It might be a writer like Shakespeare, an artist like Monet, a footballer like Thierry Henry, an actor like Tom Cruise. And you might think to yourself, 'I could never write like that, paint like that, play like that or act like that. I'd love to be able to, but I couldn't do it. I haven't got it in me.' That's how we can so easily feel, reading this sort of list – it sounds so great to able to live like that in all areas of my life, but I just can't do it. I don't feel like I've got it in me.

But suppose it was possible for the spirit of Shakespeare, or Monet, or Henry, to come and live in you and animate you. Then you could do it. So we have the Spirit of Jesus in us, animating us, leading us. He pulls us and draws us to produce his fruit. That is what the leading of the Spirit is all about – he leads us to live this way.

So to Round 1

As I said in starting this section, all of this means that for the Christian there is going to be a fight. We've spoken of the pull of

the sinful nature, which leads us towards evil, and now of the pull
of the Spirit, who leads us towards good. Remember verse 17 said
that they are 'in conflict with each other'. These two are enemies,
and so, once the Spirit gets into the ring, it's Round 1 and the fight
begins. The Spirit and the sinful nature are now locked in conflict
over us, pulling us in different directions. It is like a tug-of-war
between them, with us in the middle, pulled in two different
directions.

Pull with the Spirit

So far we've really only laid the groundwork for Paul's main
point. What he wants to do in this passage is to encourage us to
pull with the Spirit. We're not pawns in this fight. We're not
simply pulled between these two opposing forces; rather, we join
in the fight ourselves. Paul gives a couple of commands in this
passage in Galatians 5; they come right at the start and at the end.

> So I say, live by the Spirit, and you will not gratify the desires
> of the sinful nature.
> (Verse 16)

The word Paul uses is about walking: he says 'walk by the
Spirit'. That is, live life under the influence of the Spirit, go the way
he's pulling you, and if you do that you will not gratify the desires
of the sinful nature.

> Since we live by the Spirit, let us keep in step with the Spirit.
> (Verse 25)

The idea behind the word Paul uses here is that of walking in
line with someone else's command, like soldiers keeping in step.
Have you ever played 'Follow the leader'? Someone says, 'Walk
like this', and you all have to follow in a line, walking the same
way as the leader at the front. I made the fatal mistake recently of
letting my kids have a go at being the leader, and found myself

trying to jump like a rabbit around the living room! Well, we're to play follow the leader with the Spirit. He's setting the way to go and we keep in step with his leading.

So, you see, we don't let go of our will and let him take over. There's been a consistent stream of Christian teaching that takes that sort of line. It says that the Christian life is about losing ourselves and letting God take the controls by his Spirit. And of course it sounds very spiritual – it emphasizes how we must 'surrender' to God and hand life over to him.

The attitude behind that is, of course, absolutely right. We are to surrender our sinful desires and we are to want to live life God's way. But that view doesn't understand these commands: walk by the Spirit; keep in step with the Spirit. That is telling us we have to *do* something. God doesn't lead us by taking over. That view also doesn't understand the way the Spirit works: he doesn't override our will, or negate our will; he renews our will so that we desire to live as he wants. He doesn't grab the steering wheel of our life and say, 'Get in the back, I'm driving.' Rather, he sits next to us and says, 'Go this way.' In fact, better: he gives us the desire to go the right way.

In Greek mythology the spirits of the sea were called the Sirens. They had the bodies of birds and the heads of beautiful women. These sirens lived on stretches of rocky coast and reefs and sang a beautiful song to entice sailors to them, and so the sailors were drawn to their death. However, two famous sailors managed to sail past safely.

One was Odysseus, who filled his sailors' ears with wax so that they could not hear the beautiful song, and had himself tied to the mast, so that although he could hear it he could not steer the ship towards them. He got past safely enough, but spent all his time wishing he could have gone closer. That, I think, is a picture of how some of us live the Christian life – or at least try to. We are tempted by sin; we feel the pull of the sinful nature, and if anything stops us giving in, it's external things like tying ropes around us. That's not the life led by the Spirit that God wants.

That actually hasn't resulted in any inner change in our heart or our character. It's purely prevention by constraint.

Rather, we need to look to the other sailor who managed to get past the temptations of the Sirens. He was called Orpheus. And his tactic was different. He was a musician and so he played a tune himself – a more beautiful tune than the song of the Sirens, so his sailors weren't drawn to them.

That's the picture we need. The Spirit plays us the more beautiful tune. He leads us to choose his way, rather than sin's way. He works in us and changes us so that we want to live for God and choose to do so. The life the Spirit wants to bring about is one not of external conformity but of internal transformation. That will, of course, mean we do or don't do certain things – it will show itself externally. In fact, it might result in certain practical changes that don't give us the opportunity to sin in certain ways – not staying up late flicking through the TV channels, or not flicking through magazines that we know will make us discontented and longing for a different lifestyle. But, even here, it's not just tying ropes round us. It's outer change that comes from the inner renewal of the Spirit. The challenge, then, for us, is to keep walking by the Spirit rather than by the sinful nature.

A friend once mentioned to me all the bad reasons for not sinning he was aware of in his life. I immediately recognized them in mine. They were: so that we could be pleased with our obedience; so that we wouldn't be caught; so that we wouldn't feel guilty; so that we don't let ourselves down; and so that our image remains intact. These are all bad reasons to obey – in fact, they are further works of the sinful nature. By contrast, the Spirit leads us to love God and to love obeying him. That's what walking by the Spirit involves – real inner change, not just outward conformity.

Remember which side you're on

While we are pulled in two directions, we need to remember who we really are. We are those on the Spirit's side. So Paul says in verses 24–25:

Those who belong to Christ Jesus have crucified the sinful nature with its passions and desires. Since we live by the Spirit, let us keep in step with the Spirit.

We are under new management; we are those who now belong to Jesus. We are united with him and he is our new Lord and master. We belong to him, and not to Satan and not to the sinful nature. So we now walk by his Spirit.

As those belonging to Christ, we have done away with our sinful nature; we have crucified it. We died with Christ and were raised to new life, and the sinful nature was left in the grave. So we are not now to live by it! Rather, we are those who now live by the Spirit – we've been re-created by the Spirit and given new life, and so we carry on the Christian life walking closely with the Spirit.

All of this is to say that the call in this passage to follow the Spirit and resist the sinful nature is not a call simply to follow one influence and not another, as if there are two people beckoning us. In that sense the 'tug-of-war' illustration is deficient (as all illustrations are in some way or other). Rather, this is a call to live out now who we've become – a call to live out our new identity in Christ, and our new life in the Spirit. For Christians, not to follow the Spirit is a denial of whom we belong to, a denial of the change that's taken place and a denial of the Spirit's work in us when we became Christians in the first place.

The fight continues

We are to walk by the Spirit and produce his fruit. But sin will continue to look very attractive to us because our sinful nature will stay with us until death. And once we're re-created by the Spirit, along with the temptation to sin the Spirit will always be pulling the other way, singing his song, saying, 'This way is right, follow me.' That tension, that feeling of being pulled in opposite directions, that fight, is the very nature of the ongoing Christian life.

That's well worth noting, because some people can suggest that you get to the point where you can escape the pull of the sinful nature. There have been a variety of groups through history who have given that idea. Unfortunately, it usually results in one group of people feeling proud of themselves – because they are 'free from sin' – and another group of people feeling like second-rate Christians – because they are all too well aware that they are not 'free from sin'.

This can often come about because of an emphasis on the change that has taken place when we became Christians. 'There is a new creation,' we are told; 'the old has gone, the new has come!' (2 Corinthians 5:17). And so we continue to sin only because of the ingrained ways in which we used to live. Growing in holiness now, we're told, is a matter of unlearning those bad habits of our former life, which seems to put the fight against sin on a par with 'unlearning' our bad habits in driving – enough practice and I'll get there, because there's nothing stopping me.

Now it has to be said that the New Testament does indeed teach that there has been a vital break in the power of sin over us – we can now walk by the Spirit and so not indulge the sinful nature, as we have seen. But the sinful nature remains part of who we are, even as Christians. In fact, the sinful nature will remain part of who we are until God completes his work of new creation in us with the redemption of our bodies (see for example Philippians 3:20–21; Romans 8:23).

The sixteenth-century reformer Martin Luther wrote this about the ongoing pull of the sinful nature (what he calls the 'flesh'):

> The lust of the flesh is not altogether extinct in us. It rises up again and again and wrestles with the Spirit. No flesh, not even that of the true believer, is so completely under the influence of the Spirit that it will not bite or devour, or at least neglect, the commandment of love. At the slightest

provocation it flares up, demands to be revenged, and hates a neighbour like an enemy, or at least does not love him as much as he ought to be loved.

That's the picture I think Paul paints – the sinful nature keeps on tempting us not to follow the Spirit. The result is that we will constantly be tempted not to love people as we should, or to respond badly. In fact, as Luther says, it doesn't take much provocation before we find that the sinful nature is still alive and kicking. This is not to say that there is no victory over the sinful nature – not at all. But it is to say that growing in holiness now, walking by the Spirit, is far more than unlearning my bad habits of living apart from God: it is a fight!

Fight today

Why not look through those lists in Galatians 5 again: the acts of the sinful nature and the fruit of the Spirit? Think about which areas you know you struggle in – your anger, your thoughts, your selfishness, whatever it is. Pray to God and ask him to help you listen to the Spirit and walk by the Spirit in that area.

That's a prayer we'll have to pray for the rest of our Christian lives on earth, because our sinful nature will still be here. As well as that prayer, we will also confess where we failed, and God will freely forgive us. But it's a prayer we can pray with the confidence that there is the possibility of victory. Such victory won't be sudden and it certainly won't be complete. But it will be there. It will come as we walk by the Spirit.

study 5

Galatians 5:16–26

1. What choices in how we live does Paul mention in verse 16? What does this look like in practice?
2. How has this situation come about? Is this true for everyone?
3. How will the influence of the sinful nature show itself? What surprises you about this list?
4. How does the influence of the Spirit show itself? What is significant about this list?
5. What is Paul's concern for his readers in this passage? What does he want them to do?
6. What reasons does Paul give for living by the Spirit?
7. What practical outcome does Paul see in verse 26 if they follow his commands? What practical outcomes could you see in your church situation if people did the same?
8. What attitude should we have to 'growth in godliness' from this passage? What errors does it help us avoid?
9. What does experiencing the Spirit look like from this passage?

6: Getting more of the Spirit?

Ephesians 4:1–6;
5:15–21

We have an old gas boiler in our house. The pilot light is on all the time. But the boiler is not always giving out heat and power. Some have only got the pilot light of the Holy Spirit in their lives, whereas when others are filled with the Holy Spirit, they begin to fire on all cylinders.

I wonder how you respond to that sort of statement. It might make some people feel insecure. It raises the question, 'Do I have the full power of the Spirit? Or am I running with only a pilot light? Have I been filled?' And so it could make you feel like an underpowered, second-rate Christian. Alternatively, it might make others feel excited. You think to yourself, 'Great – there's more power available. I feel like I've only got the pilot light, so I'm glad to hear there's more to come. Bring it on!' Or maybe it leaves some people feeling confused and not sure what to make of it.

One reason for our dilemma is that the Bible does speak in different ways about 'having' and 'getting more' of the Spirit. I want to argue that we are given both the reassurance that those who believe in Jesus have the Spirit in them, and the challenge to be influenced more and more by the Spirit.

There are also two distinct biblical phrases we need to look at and understand. There is the baptism of the Holy Spirit, and there is being filled with the Spirit. Unfortunately, people use these phrases in different ways, which only complicates matters. In this chapter we're going to look at these two ideas – baptism and fullness – and think about what they mean and what we should expect.

The baptism of the Spirit

I remember being on a mission trip in India with a group of Christians from a variety of backgrounds. Over coffee one evening the topic of baptism came up. One person believed that the children of Christian parents should be baptized, but that it didn't mean they were necessarily Christians or had the Holy Spirit. Someone else argued that only believers should be baptized (which ruled out the infants), but that such people already had been baptized with the Holy Spirit from the day they trusted Jesus. Finally, another put forward the view that you should come to faith first and then be baptized with water, and then, at some later point, you could be baptized with the Spirit. And this left open the threatening possibility for many in the room that, while they were Christians, they were yet to be baptized with the Spirit.

The different positions put forward that evening illustrate how the baptism of the Holy Spirit has been a source of great discussion and controversy down the years. As this is a book about the Holy Spirit rather than about who should be baptized with water, we'll focus on what baptism of the Spirit is and what it means for us today.

'I will baptize you . . . '
The phrase 'baptism of the Spirit' is found seven times in the Bible. And six of them all refer to one person saying the same thing. That is, John the Baptist speaking of Jesus. This is what he said: 'I

baptise you with water for repentance. But after me will come one who is more powerful than I, whose sandals I am not fit to carry. He will baptise you with the Holy Spirit and fire' (Matthew 3:11).

You can find the same words repeated in the other gospels (Mark 1:8; Luke 3:16; John 1:33), and they are quoted again in Acts 1:5 and 11:16. The seventh time the phrase 'baptism of the Spirit' is used is by the apostle Paul in 1 Corinthians 12:13, which we will look at later.

John's words tell us a couple of things. First, they tell about the difference between his ministry and that of Jesus. He baptized with water for repentance, whereas Jesus would baptize with the Holy Spirit. There was a qualitative difference between these two baptisms. John's seems to be more external, more of a sign of something. It represents the repentance of the people who undergo it, whereas Jesus' is going to be more internal; it will involve a transformation by the Spirit.

The promised Holy Spirit

John didn't utter these words in a vacuum. He was speaking to people who would have known their Old Testament, and so to them this mention of the Spirit would have meant something. One of the promises that God's people had looked forward to was a new activity of God by his Spirit. There were numerous references to it. God had spoken about it more than once. For example:

> 'For I will pour water on the thirsty land,
>   and streams on the dry ground;
> I will pour out my Spirit on your offspring,
>   and my blessing on your descendants.'
> (Isaiah 44:3)

> 'I will give you a new heart and put a new spirit in you; I will remove from you your heart of stone and give you a heart of flesh. And I will put my Spirit in you and move you to follow my decrees and be careful to keep my laws.'
> (Ezekiel 36:26–27)

'And afterwards,
  I will pour out my Spirit on all people.
Your sons and daughters will prophesy,
    your old men will dream dreams,
    your young men will see visions.
Even on my servants, both men and women,
    I will pour out my Spirit in those days.'
(Joel 2:28–29)

Jews read these passages and expected a time to come when God worked by his Spirit in a new way. This was connected with the idea of a new age of the Spirit in which God made a new covenant. In several of these passages a new covenant is mentioned as part of what God will do. This new covenant will replace the old covenant so that a new relationship with God will be formed. At the heart of that new relationship is the promise of this work of the Holy Spirit. This is why the Holy Spirit is referred to as 'the promised Holy Spirit' (Ephesians 1:13) and why Paul said that Christians now receive 'the promise of the Spirit' (Galatians 3:14). The Old Testament was always looking forward to the fulfilment of the promises about the Spirit.

So when John the Baptist stood up and said, 'Someone's coming after me who'll baptize you with the Holy Spirit', he meant that God was about to fulfil all these promises and he'd do it through the Messiah, Jesus. He was the one who'd bring the Spirit and baptize people in a new way.

Jesus himself spoke about these promises being fulfilled through him and showed that this great turning point in God's plans was going to come about. In John 7:37–39 we read:

On the last and greatest day of the Feast, Jesus stood and said in a loud voice, 'Let anyone who is thirsty come to me and drink. Whoever believes in me, as the Scripture has said, will have streams of living water flowing from within.' By this he meant the Spirit, whom those who believed in him were later to receive. Up to that time the Spirit had not been given, since Jesus had not yet been glorified.

Notice that Jesus says there's going to be a source of new life within us, and that it is in fulfilment of promises made in the Old Testament. John then tells us that this refers to the Holy Spirit, but the Spirit hadn't been given yet because Jesus hadn't yet died and been raised. This is why, after Jesus' death and resurrection, he was so insistent that his disciples stay in Jerusalem until they had received the Holy Spirit. So in Acts 1:4–5 we read:

> On one occasion, while he was eating with them, he gave them this command: 'Do not leave Jerusalem, but wait for the gift my Father promised, which you have heard me speak about. For John baptised with water, but in a few days you will be baptised with the Holy Spirit.'

Now this doesn't mean that the Holy Spirit wasn't doing anything up to this point in the Old Testament. In fact, we're told that the Holy Spirit taught people (Nehemiah 9:20), gifted people (Exodus 31:3), empowered people (Judges 3:10), and warned people through the prophets (Nehemiah 9:30). We're told that the Israelites could, and did, rebel against the Spirit (Psalm 106:33) and grieve the Spirit (Isaiah 63:10). We're told that it is by the Spirit that God is with his people (Haggai 2:5).

But the new age of the Spirit would see the Spirit's work *go deeper* – those verses earlier speak of an inner transformation that the Spirit brings. And the Spirit's work would *go wider* – those verses speak of his being poured on all people in the same way, rather than being limited.

The Spirit at Pentecost

This promise of the Spirit coming in a new way was what was fulfilled at Pentecost, which is described in Acts chapter 2. Luke actually uses different terms to describe this – in chapter 2 itself he says the disciples were filled with the Spirit (2:4). But it is clearly the fulfilment of the baptism with the Spirit that Jesus promised his disciples back in chapter 1: 'Do not leave Jerusalem, but wait for the gift my Father promised, which you have heard me speak about. For John baptised with water, but in a few days you will be baptised with the Holy Spirit' (verses 4–5).

That was a unique moment because this was when the Holy Spirit came in this new promised way, which is why Peter explains the event by quoting some of the verses we listed earlier, saying, 'This is what was spoken by the prophet Joel' (Acts 2:16–21). This is why the Holy Spirit came with the fireworks of flames and wind and the miracle of being able speak in other languages. This was the start of the new covenant age, as opposed to the old covenant. And Peter then stood up and told people to repent and be baptized, and he said they'd be forgiven and they would receive the Holy Spirit.

From this we should see that the Spirit is given when people trust in Jesus. 'Repent and believe,' says Peter, 'and you *will* receive the Spirit.' This fits with the idea that the Spirit is part of the promise of the new covenant.

That all those who believe in Jesus have the Spirit is clear from a few other references. For example, in Romans chapter 8 Paul says that if you don't have the Spirit in you, you don't have Christ; you're not a Christian at all. In Galatians 3 he says that we receive the Spirit when we hear the gospel with faith. So all people who believe in Jesus have the Spirit. This takes us back to our first chapter, about being born again – we're given new life by the Spirit. That is what makes us Christians at all.

So what?

The significance of receiving the Spirit is shown for us in Acts. As we are told about the spread of the gospel to different groups of people, we are taught that everyone is equal in the new covenant. We all receive the same baptism of the Spirit and so are on an equal footing in the new covenant. In other words, the narrative of Acts shows us how we are all united by our common experience of the Spirit. Let me explain how we see this in Acts and then we'll look at some other passages to help.

We saw that when the Holy Spirit came at Pentecost he came with some extraordinary signs so that there was no doubt he'd arrived. These signs occur again at a few significant moments in the rest of Acts. These are moments when a new group of people first come to believe the gospel, and the extraordinary signs of the Spirit act as a kind of authentication that they are true believers. The external signs show that they've received the promised Spirit in the same way as everyone else.

So in Acts chapter 8 the gospel comes to the Samaritans. Some people believe, but then receive the Spirit at a later point, once Peter and John have arrived. I think it happened like that because the church in Jerusalem needed to know that the Samaritans, who were sort of half-Jews and greatly disliked, were true Christians and were on a par with Jewish Christians. And so the giving of the Spirit was delayed until two of the apostles could be there and see it for themselves.

The next time we see the Spirit arrive with the obvious external signs is when the first Gentiles are converted in Acts 10. It is very instructive to see how Peter understands this as he reports it to the church in Jerusalem. In Acts 11:15–18 he says:

'As I began to speak, the Holy Spirit came on them as he had come on us at the beginning. Then I remembered what the Lord had said: "John baptised with water, but you will be baptised with the Holy Spirit." So if God gave them the same gift as he gave us, who believed in the Lord Jesus Christ, who was I to think that I could oppose God?'

When they heard this, they had no further objections and praised God, saying, 'So then, God has granted even the Gentiles repentance unto life.'

Peter sees that the Spirit comes in the same way as at Pentecost, and so he concludes that the Gentile believers were true Christians; they have the 'same gift' – they weren't to be considered second-rate or second-class Christians.

The last time this happens is when Paul meets some people in Acts 19 who are in a kind of time-warp situation. They have heard only John the Baptist's message of repentance – and so they don't know about Jesus or even that there is a Holy Spirit.

We are told of many other conversions in Acts apart from these three, and in them people come to believe the gospel and receive the Spirit immediately and without any miraculous external signs. That's what normally happens. The extraordinary stuff happens a few times to teach us about our unity in the Spirit. God makes sure that, each time a new group is included in the church, the marks of the Spirit are there just as they were for the Jews at Pentecost. That way there can be no denying our common experience and unity in the Spirit.

We can see this point spelt out for us in 1 Corinthians 12:13, where Paul talks about being baptized by the Spirit: 'For we were all baptised by one Spirit into one body – whether Jews or Gentiles, slave or free – and we were all given the one Spirit to drink.' Paul is talking about the church in this passage, and the point he is making is that everyone is part of the body, no matter how different they are, whether Jew or Gentile, or slave or free. He explains the idea of joining the body as being baptized by one Spirit into, or so as to form, one body.

This baptism means we *are* all part of the one body; you can't separate Christians into first- and second-class. He says that 'we were all given the one Spirit to drink'. There is no division in the church between those who have been given the Spirit and those who haven't. This is why Christians, or indeed anyone else, are never told to seek to be baptized by the Spirit. That is not a command to be found in the New Testament. And the reason is that, if someone believes in Jesus, that person has been baptized by the Spirit already.

Realize our unity

The baptism of the Spirit, then, means we should realize the unity between us in Christ, no matter what other differences there are between us. Christians are very different people – in age, race, culture, background, education, interests and so on. It would be very easy for the church to divide along one or other of those lines. It would be very easy for one group to look down on another, and to feel superior or inferior for some reason.

The baptism of the Spirit puts a stop to all that. We have all been given the one Spirit to drink. There is no difference between us in that sense. Preserving and living out this unity is then of great import-ance in the life of the church. So in Ephesians 4:3 Paul says: 'Make every effort to keep the unity of the Spirit through the bond of peace.'

You know the phrase 'Blood is thicker than water', which expresses the closeness of the family bond. In churches we should have the phrase 'The Spirit is thicker than blood' to express the even closer connection between all those who share the Spirit, no matter how different they are in other ways.

Be reassured

We mentioned at the start it was quite possible to feel insecure – do other people have more of the Spirit than I do? This teaching about the baptism of the Spirit means we should be reassured that if we have trusted in Jesus we have received the Spirit. And so we should relax – no-one else has 'more' of the Spirit than we do.

I was watching the film *Robots* with my kids recently. In that film the characters, who are all robots, can get 'upgrades'. They look in the shop window at the shiny new models, with all the latest features. They are envious of those who have the latest upgrades and long for them themselves.

We can get into thinking like that with the Spirit: 'God changed me a bit when I became a Christian, but he's given the latest upgrade to other people. And so I feel second-rate and as if I ought to seek out this upgrade for myself.' If that's how we think, it becomes very easy to feel insecure: 'I need the latest upgrade of the Spirit so I'll function better.' We must stop that way of thinking. If you believe in Christ then the Spirit has re-created you; he does live in you and there is no upgrade to get.

We must remember here that the Spirit is a person. The whole 'upgrade' idea slides into thinking that he's like a power I can get more of, or get more connected to. Our family recently went on holiday and my mum came along with us. If I had told you my mum was coming on holiday you wouldn't have asked me, 'How much of your mum is coming with you?' or 'Which part of your mum is coming?' We might like to choose how much of someone or which part of someone comes along, but we don't have that luxury! It's the same with the Spirit. He is a person and you have all of him or you don't have him at all. Be reassured that no-one has more of the Spirit than you do.

The filling of the Spirit

What, then, does it mean to be filled by the Spirit? We read about this in Ephesians 5:18–21 (my translation):

> Do not get drunk on wine, which results in ungodly living. Instead, be filled by the Spirit, speaking to one another with psalms, hymns and spiritual songs, singing and making music from your heart to the Lord, always giving thanks to God the Father for everything, in the name of our Lord Jesus Christ, and submitting to one another out of reverence for Christ.

In this section of Ephesians Paul is talking about how to live as a Christian. The section starts back in chapter 4 verse 17, where he says we must no longer live as non-Christians do; rather, we must be remade in the image of God. He talks about not lying or stealing, but speaking the truth and working. He covers our speech, our sex life, our relationships and so on. And notice he throws in there a reference to the Spirit in chapter 4 verse 30 – 'do not grieve the Holy

Spirit' – which we'll come back to. In chapter 5 verse 8 he comes back to the change that's happened to us in becoming Christians: we no longer live in darkness; we've been moved to the light. So we should now live as children of the light; we should be careful how we live and understand how God wants us to live.

Living out your new life

So the big picture in this section of the letter is something like this: you have changed in becoming a Christian, so now live differently. And it's in that context that he refers to being filled by the Spirit. That big picture shows us that being filled by the Spirit is to do with living out our new life as God's people. Paul hasn't suddenly changed topic here; this is about living now as God wants us to live, living in the light. Put simply, being filled by the Spirit is the way we live out this new life and change from our old way of life.

This is why I have translated this verse as 'be filled *by* the Spirit', rather than 'be filled *with* the Spirit'. (Both are possible translations, but the first is the more likely and most commentators agree that's the best way to put it.) If we say 'be filled *with* the Spirit', it sounds as though I'm the jug and the Holy Spirit is the water, and I'm being filled up with the Spirit. I get more of him – which is exactly what I've been arguing against above.

If we say 'be filled *by* the Spirit', however, I'm the jug and the Spirit wants to fill me with stuff. Paul has been talking this way already in the letter. Back in chapter 3 verse 19 he speaks about being 'filled to the measure of all the fullness of God', and in chapter 4 verse 13 he says we need to grow so that we are 'attaining to the whole measure of the fullness of Christ'. We are to become fully Christ-like, fully God-like, as he made us in his image. And the Spirit is the one who fills us with these qualities.

Under the influence

This is where the contrast with wine is helpful. 'Do not get drunk on wine, which results in ungodly living. Instead, be filled by the Spirit' (5:18, my translation).

I remember a TV programme where two teenagers were interviewed about their experience of God, and they said, 'It's great – the Holy Spirit gives us a buzz. It's better than alcohol or drugs.' And one of them mentioned that the Bible said that the Holy Spirit was better than getting drunk. She didn't quote a verse, but I presume it was this one she had in mind. Well, I hope we've seen in this book that the Spirit does indeed bring an experience, because he brings us to know Jesus, to know God as Father; he brings us to know their love and fills us with joy.

But that's not what's going on here. Paul is not talking about some alternative 'high' of the Spirit. He's thinking of two different influences and their different results. 'Do not get drunk on wine, which results in ungodly living.' The word Paul uses could be translated 'reckless living'. It sums up the way of life they have turned from, all the stuff in chapters 4 and 5 about greed, bitterness, sexual immorality and obscene talk. The influence of alcohol results in that stuff coming out. Maybe you've been to parties where people have had too much to drink, and as a result they've sworn at someone, argued with someone, hit someone, slept with someone, become obscene. Self-restraint is lost under the influence of alcohol.

Instead, Paul says, be filled by the Spirit. Let the Spirit influence you instead. The influence of the Spirit will lead in a very different direction. Instead of the old way of life, the results of the Spirit's influence are seen in the description that follows: speaking to each other, singing and making music, giving thanks and submitting to each other.

Showing the Spirit

So what will being filled by the Spirit look like? It will show itself, first, in people speaking to each other. If refers specifically to speaking to each other in songs, but I don't think it's restricted to that – that's just one good example of how we now encourage each other, and remind each other of the truth, and spur each other on.

The filling of the Spirit will be seen in how we talk to each other. We will speak truth and encourage each other. It's worth looking back to 4:29: 'Do not let any unwholesome talk come out of your mouths, but only what is helpful for building others up according to their needs, that it may benefit those who listen.'

Secondly, being filled by the Spirit shows in worshipping God – 'singing and making music from your heart to the Lord'. Spirit-filled worship isn't about a certain atmosphere or a certain type of music or anything like that. It's all about the attitude of our hearts to God. It's about sincere, heartfelt worship of God, whatever the tune and whatever the sound being made.

Thirdly, being filled by the Spirit shows itself in 'always giving thanks to God the Father for everything, in the name of our Lord Jesus Christ'. The person filled by the Spirit becomes a more grateful person. You see that effect especially, perhaps, when life is hard, and you don't want to give thanks, but you do.

Fourthly, being filled by the Spirit shows itself in submitting to each other (verse 21). We stop being domineering and arrogant. As we talk to each other we put others first in conversation rather than putting them down. We stop trying to play the 'Look at me, aren't I great?' game. And Paul goes on to talk about what that will look like between wives and husbands, and parents and children, and slaves and masters. Spirit-filled people show it in their attitude in the home and the workplace.

But in fact we shouldn't restrict the effects of being filled by the Spirit to just these things. Remember all that stuff that comes earlier in chapters 4 and 5? Getting rid of bitterness and malice, avoiding sexual immorality, being kind and forgiving and all the rest? That's all part of being filled by the Spirit as well. The big picture here is that the Spirit leads us to be more like Christ. Having re-created us, he wants to fill us with Christ-likeness. And we are to be open to his influence. We are to let him fill us in that way.

Be challenged

Unlike being baptized by the Spirit, being filled by the Spirit *is* a command to Christians. And it is no one-off experience; it's an ongoing thing. I am to be filled by the Spirit, all the time, each day. And so, if, to begin with, we were to be reassured that we have the Spirit, now we need to be challenged: does the Spirit really have me? Does he really influence me? Do I look to be filled by him, or do I ignore him?

Back in chapter 4 verse 30 we noted that we can 'grieve' the Spirit. He longs to draw us along this way, but we resist. But it's not like resisting a power, or holding back an experience. It's resisting a person and so grieving him. We can do that to the person of the Spirit. We'll think more about that in the next chapter.

study 6

Ephesians 4:1–6; 5:15–21

The first part of this chapter discussed a variety of passages. You may like to look through them as part of this study. However, the Bible study questions will focus only on two passages from Ephesians.

Read Ephesians 4:1–6

1. What is Paul's main concern in this passage?
2. What is the unity of the Spirit? How does it relate to there being 'one body and one Spirit'?
3. What does keeping the unity of the Spirit mean in practice for you?
4. What does experiencing the work of the Spirit mean from this passage?

Read Ephesians 5:15–21

5. What is the general topic Paul is talking about in this passage?
6. What comparison does he give in verse 18? What do you think the point of the comparison is?
7. What are the different results of the influence of wine as opposed to the Spirit?
8. Discuss the results of being filled with the Spirit with regard to your church. What practical differences would they make?
9. How does this differ from the way the phrase 'Spirit-filled' tends to be used today? Does that matter?
10. What does it mean to experience the Spirit from this passage?

ẍ Resisting the Spirit

Acts 6:8 – 7:60

I can clearly remember the feelings that rose up in me the time I was 'told off' at work. Someone more senior to me had sat me down and told me in no uncertain terms that I wasn't pulling my weight, that my attitude wasn't good and I needed to change. My feelings? Annoyance, anger and protest. I wanted to defend myself and hated admitting that I was in the wrong.

How do you respond in that sort of situation, when someone tells you you're wrong about something or that you have to change? If you're anything like me, you too will dig your heels in, argue your case and get a bit annoyed along the way. In other words, you will instinctively *resist*.

This is silly, really, because the correction may be extremely necessary and useful. It might be that the right reaction is gratitude to whomever gives it to us. The person who sat me down at work might have done it a little better, but the intention was good and some of the criticism was right. Unfortunately, though, the resistance route is the more common one. That's important to recognize, because in this chapter we're thinking about how we react when correction comes from God. Unfortunately, we can resist the Holy Spirit.

That is what Stephen accuses a group of in Acts chapter 7. He says to them that they 'always resist the Holy Spirit' (verse 51). It's a pretty damning charge, but it's one we have to take seriously because we are perfectly capable of doing the same.

We first meet Stephen back in chapter 6 of Acts – he's one of the people put in charge of the daily distribution of food to the widows in the church. But he doesn't just organize the food rota, important as that is; he also teaches people about Jesus (see 6:8–10).

But the group he's talking to doesn't respond very well to his teaching. He's teaching them about the change Jesus brings and so about how they need to change. And they don't like it. In fact, they hate it! So much so that Luke tells us they get Stephen on trial and persuade people to bring false charges against him. What they're doing is exactly what we mentioned earlier – digging their heels in and resisting.

Why are they so wound up?

What did Stephen say that got them reacting like this? Well, we can get some idea from verses 12–14:

> They seized Stephen and brought him before the Sanhedrin. They produced false witnesses, who testified, 'This fellow never stops speaking against this holy place and against the law. For we have heard him say that this Jesus of Nazareth will destroy this place and change the customs Moses handed down to us.'

It boils down to stuff about Moses, the law and the Temple. They accuse Stephen of saying that Jesus knocks down the pillars of Judaism. 'Jesus will destroy the Temple,' they say. 'Jesus will change the customs or laws that we received from Moses. Our faith will never be the same again!'

And of course they were right! Jesus *would* change these things because he fulfilled the law and the Temple. Take the Temple as an example. The sacrifices which were offered in the Temple were all fulfilled in Jesus; he was the once-for-all, ultimate sacrifice. And so sacrifices should no longer be offered in the Temple itself. So will Jesus of Nazareth 'destroy this place' (the Temple), as they accuse Stephen? Not in the sense that he's opposed to it at all. Stephen wasn't speaking against the Temple in that sense. But 'Yes' in that he has fulfilled it. Similarly with the law: Stephen wasn't opposed to the law, but he saw that Jesus had fulfilled it and so there would be change.

Defence becomes accusation

So how does Stephen respond to these charges? We read his defence speech in chapter 7. What he does is give them a potted history of Israel. He covers Abraham, Joseph, Moses, Joshua, David and Solomon. It's a long passage, and it needs some knowledge of Israel's history. Stephen wants to demonstrate that God has dealt with his people outside the narrow confines of Israel and Jerusalem, and that the Temple they are so concerned about can't contain God either. But his main focus and challenge concern Israel's heart attitude, and the same heart attitude of his accusers. We're going to focus on his conclusion and glance back at other parts of his speech.

Stephen draws it all together in verses 51–53 of chapter 7. Here's his conclusion on this group and what they are doing:

> 'You stiff-necked people, with uncircumcised hearts and
> ears! You are just like your ancestors: You always resist the
> Holy Spirit! Was there ever a prophet your ancestors did
> not persecute? They even killed those who predicted the

coming of the Righteous One. And now you have betrayed
and murdered him – you who have received the law
that was put into effect through angels but have not
obeyed it.'

Notice that Stephen focuses here on this group's attitude rather
than on the fulfilment we've just been talking about. He could, of
course, have spoken about that fulfilment and explained exactly
what he meant about the Temple and the law and how Jesus
changes things. But he knows that this group have heard all about
it from Peter and the others. So that's not where his focus is. His
focus is on their attitude. They don't need more explanation; they
need challenging. And so his defence becomes accusation against
them, and they are stinging words.

You see his description? They are 'stiff-necked', have 'uncircumcised' hearts and ears, and 'resist' the Holy Spirit. Those phrases
might not mean very much to us (you might be asking yourself
how exactly you might go about circumcising a heart or an ear!),
but they are all used in the Old Testament in significant places
and Stephen has already mentioned them in his history review
of Israel.

These descriptions from Stephen are basically three ways of
saying the same thing. They all focus on their attitude to God and
especially their attitude to the Holy Spirit. We'll look at the
reference to the Holy Spirit last and draw it together there. Let's
look at the other two ideas first.

Pushing off the harness
The idea of being stiff-necked is to do with an animal like an
ox or a horse which won't take a harness on its neck. As you
try to put it on, the animal stiffens and stretches its neck to resist
you. It bucks around to stop you putting it on, and, once on, it
tries to throw it off. It's a picture of an animal that won't be controlled or directed. It's the very opposite of being compliant and
submissive. That is what Stephen is saying this group are like

spiritually. As God tries to direct them and teach them and show them how to live for him, they stiffen their necks and buck in resistance.

I mentioned that these ideas were already used at significant moments in the Old Testament. The first time this term was used of Israel was just after God had rescued them from Egypt and given them his law at Mount Sinai. His people immediately made and worshipped a golden calf as a god. That's one of the incidents that Stephen tells them about in verses 40–41:

> 'They told Aaron, "Make us gods who will go before us.
> As for this fellow Moses who led us out of Egypt – we don't
> know what has happened to him!" That was the time they
> made an idol in the form of a calf. They brought sacrifices to
> it and held a celebration in honour of what their own hands
> had made.'

So as soon as God had said to them, 'Live like this', what did they do? They immediately pulled away from him, and resisted his control and direction. And what did God say about them as a result? 'I have seen these people, and they are a stiff-necked people' (Exodus 32:9).

Later on in the Old Testament, Nehemiah looks back on that event and says, 'But they, our ancestors, became arrogant and stiff-necked, and did not obey your commands' (Nehemiah 9:16). This is an attitude of arrogance as well as resistance, and it results in people disobeying God.

We can see more of this attitude when God, speaking through Jeremiah, comments on this event again:

> 'They did not listen or pay attention; instead, they followed
> the stubborn inclinations of their evil hearts. They went
> backward and not forward. From the time your ancestors left
> Egypt until now, day after day, again and again I sent you my
> servants the prophets. But they did not listen to me or pay

attention. They were stiff-necked and did more evil than their ancestors.'
(Jeremiah 7:24–26)

Notice the associated ideas: they are stubborn; they do what they want rather than what God wants; they don't listen to God or pay him any attention. That's what it means to be stiff-necked.

Putting your fingers in your ears and hardening your heart
Secondly, Stephen says, their hearts and ears are uncircumcised. It's an odd phrase to us, but the idea is that their hearts aren't open to God to obey and love him, and their ears aren't open to hear and obey his instructions.

So Jeremiah describes a group of people like this:

> To whom can I speak and give warning?
>   Who will listen to me?
> Their ears are closed
>   so that they cannot hear.
> The word of the LORD is offensive to them;
>   they find no pleasure in it.
> (Jeremiah 6:10)

See how having uncircumcised ('closed') ears means that they won't listen to God. In fact, God's words to them are offensive and they take no pleasure in them. It's a picture of people putting their fingers in their ears so that they won't listen because they don't want to have to hear and obey.

This is the description of the people of Israel after they'd received the law at Mount Sinai and were being led into the promised land. As God took them there, they wouldn't trust his word to them. Rather than being open to his promises and relying on him, they refused to listen. And this description was later applied to those who were sent into exile, who persistently refused to listen to the warnings God sent them.

That's the attitude expressed in the quotation from Amos in Acts 7:42–43:

'This agrees with what is written in the book of the prophets:

' "Did you bring me sacrifices and offerings for
forty years in the desert,
  O house of Israel?

' "You have lifted up the shrine of Molech
  and the star of your god Rephan,
the idols you made to worship.
    Therefore I will send you into exile" beyond Babylon.'

Amos's words were written to a group being threatened with exile. And in speaking to them Amos looks back to the bunch who closed their hearts and ears to God all those years earlier in the wilderness on their way to the promised land, and he says sarcastically, 'Did you offer me sacrifices then, in the desert?' No, you didn't. What you did was refuse to listen to me and worship other gods instead. And you're doing the same thing today in worshipping Molech.

So you can see that really it's the same attitude as being stiff-necked. In fact, the two ideas are sometimes linked. Moses tells people, 'Circumcise your hearts, therefore, and do not be stiff-necked any longer' (Deuteronomy 10:16).

Fighting the Spirit
Thirdly, Stephen says, 'You always resist the Holy Spirit' (verse 51). The word he uses could be translated 'fight against' or 'oppose'. The Holy Spirit is trying to do something and you fight against him. The Holy Spirit tries to lead you and get you to go this way, but you oppose him and pull in the opposite direction.

This word is again used in the Old Testament of the people who rebelled against God in the desert after the exodus from Egypt. That moment in Israel's history was the archetypal moment of resistance. Psalm 106:32–33 describes it like this:

> By the waters of Meribah they angered the LORD,
>   and trouble came to Moses because of them;
> for they rebelled against the Spirit of God,
>   and rash words came from Moses' lips.

The 'waters of Meribah' was the place where the people complained against God once again and so showed that they wouldn't trust him. The psalmist describes it as *rebelling* against the Spirit.

Isaiah looks back at the same events and says this:

> In his love and mercy he redeemed them;
>   he lifted them up and carried them
>   all the days of old.
>
> Yet they rebelled
>   and grieved his Holy Spirit.
> So he turned and became their enemy
>   and he himself fought against them.
> (Isaiah 63:9–10)

There is great tragedy in these verses: God had acted for Israel – in his love and mercy he'd redeemed them. He had been kind and gentle to them; he'd lifted them up and carried them. And what was Israel's response? To rebel and grieve his Spirit. That is, to turn against the Spirit and cause him pain and sadness. It has the idea of a parent dealing lovingly with their children, but the children being ungrateful and turning against the parent.

Why the Spirit?

As I said above, these three descriptions are really three sides of the same coin. It's a picture of people opposed to God, who will not listen to him or obey him, but rather resist him. The overriding picture is that of resisting the Spirit. The reason is what we've seen so far in this book. The Spirit is God's agent in the world – he is the member of the Godhead who works in our hearts and minds, teaching us, convicting us, leading us and empowering us. When we say, 'God is at work in someone', that's fine, but it's more precise to say, 'God is at work in him or her by his Spirit'. And so when we show all the attitudes described above, ultimately we are resisting God's Spirit at work in us.

A warning to us

These verses are a warning to us today. They warn us to beware of resisting the Holy Spirit ourselves. We need to realize that we can have the same attitude as this group did. Actually, we need to realize that this sort of attitude to God is our default position. I'm sorry to say it, but this is what is true to type. Stephen tells this group that this is what they have 'always' done – this is normal behaviour for them. So for us. This is not us on a bad day; it is us on an average day.

That this is a possibility for Christians today is made clear by Paul's command in Ephesians 4:30: 'Do not grieve the Holy Spirit.' We saw in the previous chapter that Paul is talking in that section about how we live for God, and he sees the Spirit as pulling us God's way. We, however, can resist and grieve the Spirit. We can respond in all the ways we've seen above, and, despite God's goodness and love to us, we can turn against him and cause him pain. We need to pray to God to change our hearts and to turn our hearts towards him; to pray to him to soften our hearts, to open our ears, to help us walk by his Spirit and not resist.

Resisting the Spirit – how?

We've looked at the attitude Stephen describes. But that attitude leads to certain actions which start to spell out for us what resisting the Spirit looks like in practice. You can't actually see an attitude itself – what you can see are the actions it results in. So how does resisting the Spirit show itself? Stephen tells us in verses 52–53:

> 'Was there ever a prophet your ancestors did not persecute?
> They even killed those who predicted the coming of the
> Righteous One. And now you have betrayed and murdered
> him – you who have received the law that was put into effect
> through angels but have not obeyed it.'

Shooting the messenger

First they persecute the prophets. Prophets came to speak God's Word and correct his people. Their message very often involved a rebuke, saying where the people were wrong, telling them to stop doing this or start doing that. And Israel reacted pretty badly to that sort of correction. It's not surprising, is it? If your attitude to God is what we've just described, when someone turns up to tell you what God wants, you reject the messenger.

For Israel, that was the prophets, whom they persecuted and sometimes killed. For this group in Acts 7, it was Stephen himself, who was speaking God's Word to them, then and there, and whom they then dragged out of the city and stoned.

What will it look like for us? Think back to when people have corrected you about something, or rebuked you, no matter how gently. Didn't you feel the temptation to dismiss what they said and to shun them, to think badly of them, even to speak badly of them? We too show our resistance to the Spirit by rejecting the messenger.

I remember a time when I stopped someone from being baptized. It's a long story, but someone had asked to be baptized, and all was fine, until I was informed that she was sleeping with her boyfriend. What to do? Well, first, to ask gently and find out what she understood about the Bible's teaching on sex in marriage and so on. She knew what the Bible said, but thought she didn't have to abide by that. We pressed her to reconsider – she refused. And so we said we wouldn't baptize her.

My name was mud. I was labelled by some as a pedantic fundamentalist. There was a sense, then, in which I and others involved were rejected as messengers of God's Word. Of course, I know the same temptation to reject those who challenge me, even if it's as simple as writing them off in my mind so that I don't have to consider what they say. Beware of rejecting the messenger; it's one of the things we do when we're resisting the Spirit.

Despising God's Word

Closely linked with rejecting the messenger is another symptom of resisting the Spirit; that is, rejecting God's Word to us. Stephen describes this group as those 'who have received the law that was given through angels but have not obeyed it' (verse 53).

This is looking back to when they received the law, God's Word, on Mount Sinai. It has the sense that they thought highly of the law. They said, 'This is God's Word. He gave it to us through angels. This is precious.' But then they didn't do what it said. It's a bit like the person who speaks highly of the Highway Code. He says what a wonderful thing it is, and how it keeps us all safe and how it ought to be followed by everyone. But then he doesn't keep it himself!

I think it's significant that Stephen quoted from Isaiah back in verses 49–50:

'Heaven is my throne,
    and the earth is my footstool.
What kind of house will you build for me?
                                    says the Lord.
    Or where will my resting place be?
Has not my hand made all these things?'

He's obviously making a point about how God is not limited to the Temple. But in its context that quotation is about people's attitude to God's Word. The next words in Isaiah (66:1–2) are, 'These are the ones I esteem: those who are humble and contrite in spirit, and tremble at my word' – as opposed to those who are proud and arrogant and disobey him.

So we can tell when we are resisting the Spirit by our attitude to God's Word. We know something is wrong. We know we shouldn't do it. But we do it anyway. We might even do it while speaking highly of God's Word at the same time. We might even be committed in other areas of our life. But we are still resisting the Spirit.

I think in this instance of the young woman who agreed with me that God's Word said Christians shouldn't marry non-Christians, but then said she thought it was OK in this case. She would have been thought of by her friends as a very committed person, even a very spiritual person. But I would say she was resisting the Spirit. Or I think of the friend who knows he drinks a little too much, but he laughs it off, saying, 'I know I shouldn't, but it's my only vice.' As if that's OK, then. No, it's not OK. In fact, it reveals a deeply worrying attitude to the Holy Spirit.

The Spirit is the one who brought God's Word in the first place, and he is the one who continues to speak God's Word to us. And so we shouldn't be surprised that resistance to the person of the Spirit shows itself in resisting his Word. What's worrying is that we have often separated Word and Spirit. And hence people have sometimes said that the Spirit is 'leading' them to do something, even when the Word contradicts it. This separation has been used to justify leaving a husband or wife, engaging in a variety of sexual activities including homosexual relationships, dividing churches, failing to care for family members and so on. Some of the worst blights on the church's reputation have been justified by saying we need to follow the Spirit. And, despite the spiritual language of 'being led', I'm sorry to say that in these cases it is simply a cover for resisting the Spirit.

Put more positively, a desire to be led by the Spirit will of course result in a greater desire to obey God's Word. It will result in a humility and respect before his Word, a desire that the Spirit would speak to us through it and empower us to obey it.

Rejecting God's saviour

This resistance shows itself in one last way. We actually reject God's saviour. You see that in Stephen's words, 'You have betrayed and murdered him [the Righteous One]' (verse 52). That's a title for Jesus. And this rejection of God's saviour picks up on a trend in the history. Stephen has already mentioned a couple of significant people that God used to save his people, but who were rejected. The most significant example is Moses in verses 23–40.

Look at verse 25, for example:

'Moses thought that his own people would realise that God was using him to rescue them, but they did not.'

In fact, they said to him, 'Who made you ruler and judge over us?' (verse 27). That is picked up again in verse 35, after God had appeared to Moses and told him he would rescue his people through him:

'This is the same Moses whom they had rejected with the words, "Who made you ruler and judge?" He was sent to be their ruler and deliverer by God himself, through the angel who appeared to him in the bush.'

Moses was God's chosen saviour but they rejected him. And so when Moses says that God will send 'a prophet like me' (verse 37), what do you think people will do with him? They'll do the same thing – they'll reject him. And so they did with Jesus.

This fundamental attitude of resistance and opposition not only results in rejecting God when he speaks to us; it also means we reject him when he tries to save us. It's a bit like the teenager who rejects his parents' advice and then rebels at their discipline. He even rejects them when they come to help. They come to bail him out of the prison cell, but he won't have it and refuses their aid. It shows a deep-seated rejection and an attitude of pride and arrogance.

So Stephen says to his listeners that they should be accepting Jesus as the Messiah along with the fulfilment he brings. The reason they are not is that they won't bow to God. They are resisting his Spirit.

And so God warns us. That's the most worrying thing about this. You see, it's not that rejecting God's messengers or words and being saved are two completely different things. They are in fact part of the same attitude. So I worry for those people I mentioned earlier who showed signs of resistance – I worry that ultimately they may reject Jesus.

Blasphemy against the Holy Spirit

This brings us to the sobering idea that Jesus spoke about – the unforgivable sin of blasphemy against the Spirit. We read about it in Mark 3:22–30, where the Jewish teachers of the law are accusing Jesus of having an evil spirit by which he is casting out demons.

Jesus explains that if he's casting out demons it must mean he is stronger than Satan, but then he goes on to warn them that they are in danger of putting themselves beyond the reach of forgiveness. He says that 'people will be forgiven all their sins and all the blasphemies they utter. But whoever blasphemes against the Holy Spirit will never be forgiven, but is guilty of an eternal sin.'

What were they doing that put them in such a dangerous position? Mark tells us that this is all tied up with their accusation of Jesus; he adds the comment: 'He said this because they were saying, "He has an evil spirit" ' (verse 30). What they were doing was seeing the work of the Holy Spirit in front of their eyes, seeing Jesus releasing people from Satan by the power of the Holy Spirit.

But, rather than recognizing that, they denied that that was what was happening.

So they are denying the truth of the salvation that Jesus is bringing. In one sense that's what all people who don't believe are doing. All non-Christians reject the truth of Jesus' work of salvation, and there is nothing eternally condemning about that – which is why Jesus says blasphemy against him will be forgiven.

What is different about blasphemy against the Holy Spirit is that they have seen and experienced the reality of Jesus' saving work. They've seen the Holy Spirit at work in undeniable ways and then they decide to reject the truth.

In each of the places where the Bible talks about placing yourself beyond forgiveness, this is the sort of pattern we see. It deals with people who have a clear knowledge of the truth, who in some way have tasted something of it, have seen its reality, and then have decided to reject it.

Think for example of the apostle Paul. He was pretty opposed to Jesus at one time. He was dedicated to eliminating Christians! But none of that was unforgivable. However, suppose, after his Damascus-road experience, where he saw the truth of the gospel and experienced something of Christ, he had then rejected it. That, I think, would have been blaspheming the Holy Spirit. That's an eternal sin – not eternal in the sense that it's so bad you can never be forgiven for it, but eternal in that by its nature you don't repent from it.

And it still happens today. People get close to Jesus, the Holy Spirit brings conviction and understanding, but then they reject it and oppose it. A wonderful bishop in the nineteenth century, called J. C. Ryle, said about this, 'There is such a thing as a sin which is never forgiven. But those who are troubled about it are most unlikely to have committed it.'

I think he's right. If you are concerned about this, then you aren't guilty of it, because blasphemy of the Spirit is a conscious rejection of the truth, knowing the reality of the salvation Jesus brings and opposing it. We don't know if the teachers of the law

Jesus is talking to had actually done this themselves yet. But they are clearly getting close, and that's why Jesus warns them.

God is at work in us by his Spirit. The Spirit wants to bring us to faith in Jesus; he wants to bring us to know God; he wants to teach us and lead us. Go with him – don't resist him.

study 7

Acts 7:51–53

1. Stephen describes his listeners in three ways. Look up the following references from the Old Testament and give a brief description of what the following terms mean in your own words.
   - 'stiff-necked': Exodus 32:7–9; Nehemiah 9:13–18
   - 'uncircumcised hearts and ears': Jeremiah 6:10; Deuteronomy 10:12–16
   - 'resist the Holy Spirit': Psalm 106:32–33; Isaiah 63:7–10
2. How does Stephen say this resistance to the Spirit showed itself?
3. In what different ways will this same attitude of resistance show itself today? How might it be shown by Christians as well as non-Christians?
4. Why does Paul specifically refer to resisting the Spirit rather than resisting 'God'?
5. Paul refers to grieving the Spirit in Ephesians 4:30. What does he mean by this? (Look at the surrounding verses to get the context.)
6. What challenges you most from this study? How do you want to pray in the light of it?
7. What does experiencing the Spirit look like from this passage?

6: The gifts of the Spirit

1 Corinthians 12:1–11

When I spoke on the topic of the gifts of the Spirit at our church a while ago, I began by asking people what questions they had about it. Here are some of the questions they had:

'Is the gift of tongues around today?'

'How do I know which gifts I have?'

'What is the gift of prophecy?'

'How do I receive a gift from God?'

'How do gifts relate to our natural talents?'

'Should we expect gifts of healing today?'

'How should the gifts be used in the life of the church?'

'How do you know if someone really has a gift or is just making it up?'

'What about if you feel as if you haven't got a gift?'

'Can you lose a gift?'

That list reveals something of the complexity of the topic. I have to start by telling you that it would be impossible to discuss all the issues involved in this one chapter. Entire books have been written both on the gifts in general and even on one or two of them in particular, and so I'm not going try to answer many of the questions above. (Books that explore these issues in more detail are mentioned in the 'Further reading' section if you are interested in following this up.)

What I will try to do is give the big picture on the gifts of the Spirit and hopefully lay a foundation for any further thinking and reading you do.

We each have a gift to build the church

We'll begin by looking at 1 Corinthians 12:7–11:

> Now to each one the manifestation of the Spirit is given for the common good. To one there is given through the Spirit the message of wisdom, to another the message of knowledge by means of the same Spirit, to another faith by the same Spirit, to another gifts of healing by that one Spirit, to another miraculous powers, to another prophecy, to another distinguishing between spirits, to another speaking in different kinds of tongues, and to still another the interpretation of tongues. All these are the work of one and the same Spirit, and he gives them to each one, just as he determines.

The first phrase there is slightly odd – 'the manifestation of the Spirit'. That is simply a way of saying how the Spirit shows himself ('manifests himself'). And in this passage the way he does that is by giving gifts to people. The Spirit shows himself in each Christian by giving him or her a gift of some kind.

So the first thing to notice is that *we each have a gift*. Verse 7 says the manifestation of the Spirit is given 'to each one'; similarly, verse 11 says the work of the Spirit is given 'to each one'. Every Christian has been given a gift from God by the Spirit.

We see the same thing elsewhere. For example, Peter clearly assumes that each person has received a gift when he says, 'Each of you should use whatever gift you have received to serve others, faithfully administering God's grace in its various forms' (1 Peter 4:10).

So we each have a gift from the Spirit.

The second thing to see is why the Spirit gifts each person – he does it *to build the church*. A few different pictures are used to teach us this. Back in verse 7 of 1 Corinthians 12 we're told that the manifestation of the Spirit is given for 'the common good'; that is, for the good of everyone else in the church.

Later on, in chapter 14, Paul says that gifts are given so that the church may be built up (14:5). It's a construction idea. There's a house being built down my road at the moment. Each time I pass it I glance across and see that another course of bricks has been put on; the building is rising higher and moving towards completion. The same is to be happening in the church. We are increasingly to become what God wants us to be, and the gifts of the Spirit are the tools that God puts into our hands for that building work.

Ephesians 4:16 also uses that construction word but mixes it with the organic picture of the growth of a person or a plant: 'the body ... grows and builds itself up in love, as each part does its work.' Similarly, in Romans 1:11 Paul says he wants to see the church in Rome so that he may use some spiritual gift with them 'to make [them] strong'. The Spirit gives his gifts so that we can strengthen people, make them stronger as Christians.

So spiritual gifts are for the good of the church, to build the church, to grow the church and to strengthen the church. It reminds us that the church is not the finished article; rather, God is at work building us and maturing us. And the way God does it is by gifting us by his Spirit so that we are involved in building the body.

A great variety of gifts

I once tried my hand at a bit of carpentry and made a bookstand. It's sitting on my desk in front of me as I write this and I'm very proud of it. It's only a simple thing, but when I made it the dining room table was covered in tools: tape measure, pencil, square, chisel, hammer, screwdriver, plane, sandpaper, bench hook, saw, etc.

There was a huge range of tools even for a fairly simple project. And all of those different tools were needed for me to build it properly. It's exactly the same with the church. God is building the church; we are the different tools in his hands and the full range of different tools is needed.

This is one of Paul's main points in 1 Corinthians 12: the one Holy Spirit gives a great variety of gifts. He wants to point out the great diversity there will be in the church and tells us to expect that we will have different gifts and to rejoice in having different gifts. This is why Paul gives the lists he does in verses 8–10 and 28–30. He's making a number of points, but one of them is that there is variety here. He even asks rhetorical questions, explicitly saying that we don't all have the same gifts: Are all teachers? Do all speak in tongues? Answer: 'No.' We have different gifts.

We see the same thing in Romans 12:6–8:

We have different gifts, according to the grace given us.
If your gift is prophesying, then use it in proportion to your
faith; if it is serving, then serve; if it is teaching, then teach;
if it is encouraging, then encourage; if it is contributing to the
needs of others, then give generously; if it is leadership, then
govern diligently; if it is showing mercy, then do it cheerfully.

The Spirit's calling card

It is important to grasp this, because this means that no one gift is *the* calling card of the Spirit. You can't take one item from this list and say *this one* is the definitive marker of the Spirit at work. You can't go on to suggest that if you don't have that particular gift you might not have the Spirit.

I think that is why Paul begins as he does in verses 1–3 of 1 Corinthians 12. The great calling card of the Spirit which is the same for all people is that the Spirit leads us to see that Jesus is Lord: 'no-one can say, "Jesus is Lord," except by the Holy Spirit'. That's the work of the Spirit we've thought about already in this book – showing us Jesus and leading us to faith in him. That's the same for everyone; you do look for that as a sign of the Spirit in someone's life. But while there is this same confession from everyone by the Spirit, there is a whole variety of different gifts by the Spirit.

So we mustn't make any one gift the calling card of the Spirit. No one gift should be a marker of people's spirituality. I say that because in some quarters people continue to say that about the gift of tongues. We are told that everyone should have the gift of tongues, or everyone can have the gift of tongues.

The gift of tongues itself is, of course, debated. The majority position is that it's a kind of free-flowing speech. You sort of disengage control of your tongue – technically it's called 'glossolalia'. It's a phenomenon that's known outside Christianity; there's nothing supernatural about it in and of itself. In fact, people in other religions use it. From what Paul says in 1 Corinthians 14 it is a helpful way of praying and praising God. (The minority position on 'tongues' is that it refers to speaking in other known languages.)

But, whatever it is, saying it's *the* marker of the Spirit is unhelpful at best. And at worst it can make people doubt whether they have the Spirit at all. I remember that when I was a third-year student at university, a couple of first-year students came back from church in tears. The reason they were so upset was that they'd been told that if they didn't have the gift of tongues they didn't really have the Spirit. This sort of teaching results in great pressure to 'perform' and produce this gift – so much so that I know at least one person who successfully 'faked' speaking in tongues so as to escape a pressure situation!

By contrast, Paul uses the image of the body to counter exactly this idea in verses 15–20. The body has lots of different parts, each of which has a different function. They are very different from each other, but they are all needed and all are equally part of the body. And so none are to be made to feel that they aren't really part of the church because they don't have a particular gift.

While it is the gift of tongues that has most often been used in this way, it can be done with others. For example, in some churches there will be a right appreciation of the gift of teaching. But that can sometimes result in a culture that says 'Unless you can teach you haven't really got anything to offer us here', which can get very close to saying, 'You're not really showing the signs of the Spirit; you're not really part of us.'

This passage and the rest of the New Testament, I believe, teach us that we have different gifts, and so we mustn't make any one gift a marker of the Spirit or spirituality.

All from the same Spirit

Paul also wants to emphasize that all these different gifts are from the *same* Spirit – they have the same source. So in verse 4 he says there are different kinds of gifts but the same Spirit lies behind them. And he goes on to say (in verse 5) that those different gifts result in different kinds of service in the church, but we're all serving the same Lord. And so he goes on to say (in verse 6) that the result is that God is working in each of us in different ways, but it's the same God doing it. So behind the diversity is great unity: the different gifts come from the same Spirit; the service is all to the same Lord, and it is the same God at work in each of us.

He makes the same point in the list in verses 8–10. Notice how he says that each gift is 'through the Spirit', or 'by means of the same Spirit', or 'by that one Spirit'. It comes like a drumbeat through that list, so we can't miss the fact that these each come from one and the same Spirit. This is the note he ends the list on in verse 11: 'All these are the work of one and the same Spirit, and he gives them to each one, just as he determines.'

All gifts are valuable
This tells us that all gifts are the work of the Spirit and so there are
no useless gifts. They are all part of the Spirit's work among us
for the common good and so they are all to be valued. One of the
common value divisions we make today is to separate 'supernatural' and 'natural' gifts. Things like healing or miracles or
tongues are regarded as supernatural or extraordinary, while gifts
of administration or teaching or giving money are more natural,
ordinary things.

What can then happen is that in some churches the supernatural stuff is elevated, as if to say 'This is God *really* working'.
In other churches the natural stuff is regarded as the bread and
butter of the work of the Spirit and we shouldn't really expect
any of the supernatural. This, of course, raises a variety of
questions about expectation for healing today and so on – that's
one part of what I meant when I said at the start that there were
loads of complicating issues in this topic. However, my point
here is simply that both 'sorts' are equally gifts of the Spirit.
In fact, Paul doesn't make any such distinction, and so neither
should we.

We must regard each and every gift as coming under the same
heading: a gift from God to you by the Spirit for the good of the
church. And so we mustn't draw any lines as if some were better
than others; they are all equally the Spirit working.

Again, the image of the body teaches us this point: every gift
is needed and has its place in the body. Paul stresses this in verses
21–25, telling people that they can never look at others in the
church and at their gifts and say, 'I don't need you!' You can never
say that to anyone else in the church, no matter how 'weak' that
person's gift may appear to be. Indeed, Paul says that 'those parts
of the body that seem to be weaker are indispensable'.

You may remember the great concern over Wayne Rooney
before the 2006 World Cup. It was doubtful he'd recover in
time to be fit to play. He had broken his fourth metatarsal bone –
which is one of five relatively small bones in the foot. A pretty

small part of the body, really. You might not think it would have much effect – but it is devastating if you want to play football. Likewise, in the church, those we think of as playing only minor roles, or as less significant, are actually vital. The body won't be able to work as it's supposed to and play its game without them.

In fact, all this should mean that we don't talk about 'minor' roles in the church at all, because every different role is needed. All the gifts come from the same Spirit and are valuable. And so whatever gifting the Spirit has given you, your church needs you, because every gift is given for a purpose, every gift plays its part, every gift adds to the building project of the church.

I think about my life living for God and working as a local church pastor – I need people to encourage me, to teach me, to spur me on, to give me words of wisdom or words of warning and so on. I won't last long without other people bringing their gifts to bear in my life, and so I must value all of them. More than just individually; as churches we must value all gifts. What often happens, however, is that the culture of a church gives out subtle messages that rank gifts and make some people feel excluded or unwanted.

Having said all that, I had better give some explanation of verse 31, which talks about desiring the greater gifts, and chapter 14 verse 1, which tells us especially to desire the gift of prophecy. Those verses might sound as though there is a ranking system. Well, in these chapters, especially in chapter 14, Paul is speaking about what happens when the church gets together. His main concern is that what happens in the public gatherings of the church should result in the building of the church. And so he is concerned that what is said should be understood. That's why he places certain limits on tongues in chapter 14. So when he says they should especially desire to prophesy, I think that's because it is intelligible and helpful to people in the public setting; it's not that he thinks it is the 'super-cool' gift compared to the others. That would run against what he's been saying in chapter 12.

All gifts are gifts

Imagine opening a present and it's something really cool –
PlayStation 2 or whatever you think 'cool' is. And you say, 'I am
so great. Well done, me!' That would actually be a pretty stupid
thing to say. It was a present, and the thing about a present is that
it's a gift. And the thing about a gift is, it wasn't given because of
anything about you. A gift, assuming it truly is a gift rather than a
reward of some kind, tells you more about the person who gives it
than about the person who receives it.

The trouble is, we like to rank gifts and then to work out where
we are on the ladder. We think either 'I've got a cool gift so I'm
great', or 'I've got a rubbish gift so I'm rubbish.' But they're gifts,
and you can't be proud about a gift. As we've thought above,
there is no such thing as a rubbish gift from the Spirit.

Rather, what we ought to have is thankfulness to God that he
graciously works through us, and then humility in using whatever
gift we have: humility because we know this gift isn't because of
us, and because we know that any building of the church that God
does with it is ultimately his work. I love some words of Richard
Baxter on this. He was a minister in Kidderminster in the
seventeenth century and God worked through him amazingly –
a large proportion of the town was converted at one stage. He
reflected on what God had done and then said of himself, 'I was
but a pen in God's hand, and what praise is due a pen?' You don't
praise the pen! That's the attitude we need. We need to be
humble.

Finding my gift

Lots of people ask about how they can discover their gift. This is
closely related to another question we ought to deal with first.
That is: how many gifts are there? What some people do is to add
up all the gifts listed in the New Testament, which come to about

twenty, and then use that to create a master list which you look through to find your gift.

Along with that, some people devise a questionnaire. You answer questions where you rate yourself out of five in your preferences and enjoyment of stuff. You add up your score and at the end it tells you what gift you have, or anyway are likely to have. I don't think that sort of thing is useless; sometimes it can help people think things through. But I do think that that approach has missed something about how this works.

I think they've mistakenly concluded that we have a master list of gifts. The lists of gifts given in the New Testament are shown in Table 8.1 below. Looking through that, we find that none of the lists are the same. There is some overlap between them, but some are always missing or some more are added. I think Paul or whoever was writing was pulling out a variety of examples each time rather than trying to give us an exhaustive list. He could probably have kept going with more.

I think also there's overlap between these gifts; they're not completely discrete categories. For example, when does a word of instruction become a gift of teaching? I think there's a spectrum without clear dividing lines. It's interesting to look at how Peter refers to gifts in this regard. He gives a broad division into 'speaking' gifts and 'service' gifts, which are presumably more practical. We can divide them into broad categories like that, but dividing them up precisely beyond that becomes very hard.

The point is that I don't think you have to look through a master list to find your gift or gifts. And in fact there's nothing to say that your gifts have to stay the same: God may gift people in a certain way for an occasion but not for the long term (although that's more of an observation of mine rather than a point I can make from the Bible). I think that, instead, we need to ask ourselves, 'What can I say or what can I do that will help build the church?' I should look to build people up, so I should ask myself, 'What would encourage that person or strengthen that person in his or her situation?'

1 Corinthians 12:8–11	1 Corinthians 12:28	Romans 12:6–8	Ephesians 4:11	1 Peter 4:11
word of wisdom				
word of knowledge				
faith				
healing				
miracles	miracles			
prophecy	prophets	prophecy	prophets	
distinguishing between spirits				
tongues	tongues			
interpretation of tongues				
	apostles		apostles	
	teachers	teaching	teachers	
	administration			
	helping			
		exhortation		
		giving		
		leadership		
		showing mercy		
		service		service
			pastors	
			evangelists	
				speaking

Table 8.1 List of gifts in the New Testament

Get serving

I take it that we want churches where people are encouraged, warned, reminded, instructed, cared for, welcomed, challenged, loved, comforted and so on, so that they grow in Christ, stay loyal to him and mature in him, and so that our churches grow and mature in becoming the body Christ wants. And so we should look to do whatever would be for that 'common good'. In other words, we should look to get serving and trust that we will use our gifts as we go.

I say that also because we must remember that we have mutual responsibilities for each other as well as specific gifts. Just think, for example, of some of the commands we're given in the New Testament that we are to put into practice towards one another: love, teach, care, serve, spur on, encourage.

We should be looking to do all that stuff anyway. But, as we do it, we will find that we are particularly gifted at some elements of it. So, for example, I discovered, and people told me, that I had a gift for teaching. But I found that out only by opening my mouth in Bible studies and joining in. You may find you have a gift of encouragement. But you'll discover that only by talking to people and looking to encourage them. I take it there's a challenge for some of us there: how will you know if you have a gift of healing? I presume it will be by praying for healing. And for some of us there may be areas we are tempted to avoid.

Loving relationships

I hope you see where we've got to so far: we each have a gift from the Spirit that we are to use for the building of the church; there'll be a variety of gifts, they're all valuable, and we're to remember they're gifts. There's one more aspect of this we must get right if the Spirit is to work through us as he wants to. That's to do not with gifts themselves but with the relationships between us.

Sometimes people take this idea of gifting in the church and illustrate it with the picture of a well-running machine. We are each a cog or whatever in the machine. We each play our part and the machine runs smoothly. But that depersonalizes it. You don't just press the 'on' switch and use your gift. We must think of gifts as happening in relationships. They are functions of the body to each other, and we are all members of the body. And so they are things we do as we relate to each other. The picture isn't of a machine running well; it's much more of a family building each other up, caring for each other, teaching each other and so on. This is profoundly relational.

And so it gets worked out in relationships. Some of it does get worked out in larger meetings, which is why we should want a variety of people to contribute to our larger church gatherings. But then much of it will get worked out in small groups in the church, precisely because that's where we develop closer relationships and all have more opportunity to contribute. And much of it will get worked out just within relationships in the church as we interact, and won't be part of any official 'meeting time'. For example, I think many words of wisdom will be spoken as we ask someone for advice. Much of this will be relatively unseen: the meal dropped round, the visit in hospital with an encouraging word, the behind-the-scenes organization.

But as well as *where* this happens, we must think about *how* this happens. This is why Paul spends chapter 13 of 1 Corinthians talking about love. Just look at the first verses:

If I speak in human or angelic tongues, but have not love,
I am only a resounding gong or a clanging cymbal. If I have
the gift of prophecy and can fathom all mysteries and all
knowledge, and if I have a faith that can move mountains,
but have not love, I am nothing. If I give all I possess to the
poor and surrender my body [to hardship], but have not
love, I gain nothing.
(1 Corinthians 13:1–3)

I could be a very able teacher, but if I don't come to my church looking to teach in love, I may as well stay at home. You could be the most sacrificial giver, but if you don't do it in love, it's wasted. Gifts aren't like part of a machine that will just 'work' when you press the button; they are like tools in our hands that can be used well or badly, all depending on us and our attitude. There is nothing spiritual about very gifted people using their gifts in an unloving way.

1 Corinthians 13 is often read at weddings, and not surprisingly, because it gives such a wonderful description of love. But here in 1 Corinthians it is a rebuke to this church, whose members are not loving each other. They're more concerned about using their gifts to perform on the stage and get applause, whether it is benefiting other people or not. We must beware. Gifts are used in relationship with each other, but they must be loving relationships.

So the Spirit equips us, gifts us to build the church. God puts tools in our hands for the good of the rest of the family. So living by the Spirit will mean serving each other with whatever gift we've received, and doing so in love.

study 8

1 Corinthians 12:1–11

1. What is the prime work of the Spirit for everyone, from verses 1–3?
2. What is Paul's point in verses 4–6?
3. What do we learn about the purpose of the Spirit's gifts from verse 7? Explain the purpose of the gifts in your own words with regard to your church.
4. What is Paul trying to emphasize in verses 8–11? Why is he emphasizing this?
5. What attitude should we have to our own gifts?
6. What attitude should we have to other people's gifts?
7. How can you use your gifts more in your church?
8. With what attitude must gifts be used? (See 1 Corinthians 13.)
9. What does experiencing the work of the Spirit look like from this passage?

9: Empowered by the Spirit

The book of Acts

We had a training seminar on evangelism in our lounge recently. The person leading it asked the group what they found difficult in telling the gospel to friends, family and colleagues. A variety of answers were written up on a flip chart. One was echoed several times and was very challenging. It was that we were scared – scared of what people would think, scared of what would happen to the relationship, scared we wouldn't know what to say, scared we wouldn't answer their questions. Scared.

The book of Acts is all about the spread of the gospel. Luke gives us regular summary phrases just to remind us of this point; every so often he says something like, 'So the word of God spread' (6:7) or 'The word of the Lord spread widely and grew in power' (19:20).

Luke also makes it clear why the gospel spread in this way. It was obviously through the efforts of the apostles and others who became Christians. But, while it was through them, they weren't the real reason. It wasn't down to their energy and initiative. Rather, it was down to the empowering of the Holy Spirit.

Filled with the Spirit – to speak for Jesus

We see an example of this in Acts 4:5–13. Just before the events of this passage, Peter had healed a cripple and then preached a sermon about Jesus. The religious leaders, called the Sanhedrin, got pretty troubled about this, and as a quick solution they threw Peter and John in jail for the night. The next day they were brought out for a kind of trial in front of all these religious leaders. Remember that Peter and John were fishermen by background, and they were now facing a bunch of theological bigwigs. This would have been a daunting moment for them. Here's what happened:

> The next day the rulers, elders, and the teachers of the law met in Jerusalem. Annas the high priest was there, and so were Caiaphas, John, Alexander and others of the high priest's family. They had Peter and John brought before them and began to question them: 'By what power or what name did you do this?'
>
> Then Peter, filled with the Holy Spirit, said to them: 'Rulers and elders of the people! If we are being called to account today for an act of kindness shown to a cripple and are asked how he was healed, then know this, you and all the people of Israel: It is by the name of Jesus Christ of Nazareth, whom you crucified but whom God raised from the dead, that this man stands before you healed. He is
>
> > ' "the stone you builders rejected,
> >   which has become the cornerstone."
>
> 'Salvation is found in no-one else, for there is no other name given under heaven by which we must be saved.'
>
> When they saw the courage of Peter and John and realised that they were unschooled, ordinary men, they were astonished and they took note that these men had been with Jesus.

Peter is bold and courageous. He could have played it down – mentioned Jesus perhaps, but only briefly. Instead, he takes them on and goes further than their question asked. They are astonished at the courage of these men.

But notice where this courage comes from. Luke told us in verse 8 that 'Peter, *filled with the Holy Spirit*, said to them...' The Holy Spirit filled Peter at that moment so that he was empowered to respond in that way.

There is a strong link in the Bible between the Spirit and speaking the words of God. We even see it in the ministry of Jesus himself. He read in the synagogue from Isaiah 61:1–2, saying,

> The Spirit of the Lord is on me,
>   Because he has anointed me
>   To preach good news to the poor.
> (Luke 4:18)

Similarly, in John 3:34 he says that he speaks the words of God because God has given him the Spirit without limit.

There are other examples of this for people in Acts as well. In chapter 4 verse 31 we read: 'After they prayed, the place where they were meeting was shaken. And they were all filled with the Holy Spirit and spoke the word of God boldly.'

This comes at the end of a prayer meeting which had been called because of the threats of the Sanhedrin. Their prayer expresses their utter dependence on God for the advance of the gospel. And, having prayed, they are filled with the Spirit and then speak the word of God boldly. The Spirit's filling is what empowers them to speak. He gives them boldness in the face of the threats.

Later on, we are told that Stephen was not only given boldness by the Spirit but he was also given wisdom by the Spirit – so that he knew what to say to people (6:10).

All these references show us that the person empowered by the Spirit shows it by *speaking*. They speak the gospel to people even when afraid. They speak boldly and they speak wisely. The Spirit shows himself by empowering us to speak.

I don't know about you, but I usually feel the temptation not to speak the gospel. I often feel the pressure of disapproval of those around me; they don't have to threaten me with anything more than a glance or a raised eyebrow. And so I need to pray to God for the strengthening of the Spirit and trust that as I try to speak he will empower me to speak boldly. In the same way, I often feel as if I don't know what to say and again need to pray for wisdom from the Spirit. I should still do helpful things like learning a gospel outline – it simply means that I look to God to help me by his Spirit as I speak.

We need to note, then, that this meaning of the phrase 'filled with the Spirit' is different from that which we saw in a previous chapter. That shouldn't trouble us. Several phrases in the Bible have different meanings in different contexts. In the book of Acts, the writer, Luke, sometimes uses this phrase to describe someone's character, rather like the way Paul use the phrase in Ephesians 4 (for example, Acts 6:3–5; 11:24). But he also uses it in this way about the Holy Spirit filling someone at a particular moment for a particular task, as in the examples above (see also Acts 6:10; 7:55; 13:9).

This is, of course, only what Jesus had promised his disciples. Luke 12:11–12 says, 'When you are brought before synagogues, rulers and authorities, do not worry about how you will defend yourselves or what you will say, for the Holy Spirit will teach you at that time what you should say.' So a specific ministry of the Holy Spirit is to empower us to speak for Jesus.

I think there is a great variety among us in how this will show itself. Some people are especially gifted at speaking about Jesus to others, so much so that it seems to come completely naturally to them and they seem to love nothing more than witnessing. By comparison, I remember the story of a student who was very shy and nervous of speaking to anyone about his faith. However, he really wanted his friends to understand the good news about Jesus. And so he thought he would invite one of his friends to a talk.

Even this was a tall order for him. He had to work really hard to summon up the confidence to call round on his friend with an invitation in his hand and knock on the door. And when his friend answered it, he was so nervous he couldn't bring himself to say anything. In the end he simply thrust the invitation into his friend's hand and ran for it!

I'm not suggesting that's ideal, but I do think that is still an example of the empowering of the Spirit. He was helped to do something he wouldn't otherwise have done, and had the concern and conviction to do something. For him it was big step. I hope that over time and with more empowering of the Spirit he will be able to say something.

So we mustn't think this empowering will mean we are all made into Billy Graham types, ready and able to preach. It will look different for each of us, and our different personalities and gifts aren't overridden. But for all of us the Spirit wants to empower us so we can speak the word of God boldly.

The Holy Spirit – director of missions

We see more of the work of the Holy Spirit in evangelism later on in the book of Acts. In chapter 13 it is the Holy Spirit who kicks off the first missionary journey.

> In the church at Antioch there were prophets and teachers: Barnabas, Simeon called Niger, Lucius of Cyrene, Manaen (who had been brought up with Herod the tetrarch) and Saul. While they were worshipping the Lord and fasting, the Holy Spirit said, 'Set apart for me Barnabas and Saul for the work to which I have called them.' So after they had fasted and prayed, they placed their hands on them and sent them off.

We don't know how the Holy Spirit spoke – it was most likely through a prophecy – but he is the one behind it. And just in case we missed the point, two verses later Luke tells us that Paul and Barnabas are 'sent on their way by the Holy Spirit' (13:4).

Now we must notice that there is something unique about this event. This is the first ever missionary journey, and it is undertaken by Paul, to whom God has specifically given the task of taking the gospel to the Gentiles as well as to the Jews. (We read about Paul's job description in 9:15–16.) Now is the time for that special task to begin, and the Holy Spirit gets them going. So we mustn't assume we will all get a specific word of direction from the Spirit. But it does show us that the Spirit is behind mission. He not only gives us courage and wisdom as we speak; he also prompts us into speaking in the first place.

We see a similar example of the Spirit directing evangelism in 16:6–10:

> Paul and his companions travelled throughout the region
> of Phrygia and Galatia, having been kept by the Holy Spirit
> from preaching the word in the province of Asia. When they
> came to the border of Mysia, they tried to enter Bithynia,
> but the Spirit of Jesus would not allow them to. So they
> passed by Mysia and went down to Troas. During the night
> Paul had a vision of a man of Macedonia standing and
> begging him, 'Come over to Macedonia and help us.' After
> Paul had seen the vision, we got ready at once to leave for
> Macedonia, concluding that God had called us to preach the
> gospel to them.

To understand this, we need to know a little bit about the geography. They begin somewhere in what is central Turkey today. And we're told they are there because they had been kept by the Holy Spirit from preaching the word in the province of Asia, which is to the south-west. We're not told how the Holy Spirit kept them – perhaps an inner conviction they shouldn't go, a word of prophecy, a transportation problem? We don't know.

And so they try going north-east into Bithynia. But again we're told the Spirit does not allow them to. And so they can either turn round and go home (not an option) or go straight on down to Troas, which is a port on the coast. While there, Paul has this vision of a man from Macedonia, which is modern Greece, opposite Troas. And so through the combination of the road blocks and the vision, it is pretty clear where God wants them to go.

Guidance by the Spirit?

I'm currently involved in leading a church plant. When we were thinking of planting a church, there was the obvious question of where it should be. I remember that this passage from Acts was mentioned more than once during those discussions. And you can see why – it seems to be a clear example of guidance by the Spirit in mission. I think it's worth taking a moment to think about exactly what this passage teaches us about the Spirit guiding us.

First, it is obviously about guidance; God is guiding Paul and the others as to where their trip should go. The more precise question we should have in our mind is, 'Is this an example of normal guidance for us?' In other words, should it have been mentioned in our discussions about where to plant a church?

I think the answer is 'yes' and 'no'. I say 'no' because this isn't the standard way people made decisions, even in the book of Acts. If you read through Acts you'll see God directing people miraculously a number of times, often specifically linked with the Holy Spirit. For example, in 8:29 the Holy Spirit tells Philip where to stand.

But most decisions are made without any such miraculous prompting. Just glancing back through the verses before this passage, we see that Paul and Barnabas decided to start their second journey, and Paul chose to take Silas and then Timothy with him. They went on to decide to go into the region of Phrygia and Galatia (while Barnabas and Mark decided to go to Crete). They then chose to try to go south-west and then north-east. All of those are decisions made without any guidance from the Spirit.

In fact, if we look through all the decisions made in the whole book, we'll find that those that are 'Spirit-led' are very rare indeed. So the reason I say 'no' to our question, 'Is this an example of normal guidance for us?', is that it isn't an example of *normal* guidance for them.

It seems to me that their approach was to press on, making decisions that seemed wise and good. They said to themselves, 'Let's have a second journey; let's go over here or there.' And the special guidance they received came unsought, while pressing on. They didn't wait for it, or look for it.

And so I think that's how we should live – making decisions that seem wise and good in the light of God's priorities. That's why we thought of doing a church plant, and we went on to look at our city and where our congregation lived, and where other churches were and so on, and made a decision as to where it should be. We didn't need to wait for a vision.

But I also said 'yes' to that question. And I mean 'yes' in the sense that, just as God obviously wanted to push these guys in one particular direction, so he may choose to do today in some situations. We shouldn't say, 'God doesn't ever do this any more.' In fact, there are examples people can give where he clearly appears to have done so.

So I think we press on in life, making decisions in the light of God's priorities. We do so humbly, and we ask God for wisdom. And we trust that if God wishes to direct especially, he'll do so, and we should be open to that. But we don't wait for it, and we don't worry if it doesn't happen.

What we do learn, though, is that the Spirit is keen on evangelism. Virtually all of his specific moments of guidance in the book of Acts are so that the gospel goes forward. So we should expect the Spirit to give us a concern for evangelism and mission, boldness in it, and at times specific guidance for it.

'You will receive power' – signs and wonders?

We've seen the Spirit empowering us for evangelism in giving us boldness and words to say. But what about real power? In Acts 1:8 Jesus told his apostles that they would 'receive power' when the Holy Spirit came on them and they would be his witnesses. Many have said that the power Jesus was talking about was more than what we've spoken of so far.

Twenty years ago a book was written by John Wimber, called *Power Evangelism*. It created something of a storm of controversy at the time. I remember going to a conference a few years after it was published; there was a seminar on 'signs and wonders', which, to be honest, I'd never heard of before. The seminar was responding specifically to John Wimber's book.

Now the book said many things that were fine, some that were debatable, and some that, to my mind, were quite simply awful. Some of the awful things were:

- If you haven't had signs and wonders as part of becoming a Christian, then you had an inadequate conversion experience that will retard your growth as a Christian.
- Those who didn't use signs and wonders in evangelism were relying on a pre-packaged message rather than relying on God.
- Healing was available for people today and if people weren't healed it was most likely because they didn't have faith.

Now John Wimber may have later changed his mind on all those things before he died. I mention them simply to illustrate that as soon as you mention 'signs and wonders' you open a very big can of worms. We're not going to try to cover all those issues in the rest of this chapter, but because we are thinking about the Holy Spirit and evangelism we need to think at least briefly about this 'power'.

The big picture

'Signs and wonders' is a phrase we find through the Bible in both the Old and the New Testament. Calling them 'wonders' tells us that the events in question were amazing. In Acts they are mainly healings, but it could include other miracles like the plagues in Egypt. Calling them 'signs' tells us these events were significant. A sign points you to something. And that very fact tells us straight away that these miraculous events aren't ends in themselves. They are significant in what they point us to.

In the Old Testament, signs and wonders are mainly tied to the exodus, when God rescued his people from Egypt. For example, Deuteronomy 26:8 says, 'So the LORD brought us out of Egypt with a mighty hand and an outstretched arm, with great terror and with miraculous signs and wonders.'

These signs and wonders happen as part of the rescue and they are then something people should look back to as evidence of what God has done (see Exodus 10:2). They are also linked with the person performing them. At the exodus that person is Moses, and the signs show the people that God really is with him and is using him.

We see the same thing with some of the prophets, like Elijah and Elisha, who performed signs and wonders to prove that their ministry was from God. There are some other occasions in the Old Testament where God performed miraculous signs (e.g. Daniel 6:27), but most of them are linked with either the exodus or the work of specific prophets.

In the New Testament signs and wonders are linked first with Jesus. So Peter says of Jesus: 'People of Israel, listen to this: Jesus of Nazareth was a man accredited by God to you by miracles, wonders and signs, which God did among you through him, as you yourselves know' (Acts 2:22).

Jesus himself referred to these miracles, saying that they were the sign that God was really with him (John 10:38) and that they showed that God's kingdom had arrived in him (see Matthew 12:28).

And then in the book of Acts we're told that signs and wonders are done by the apostles. For example: 'The apostles performed many miraculous signs and wonders among the people ... people brought the sick into the streets and laid them on beds and mats so that at least Peter's shadow might fall on some of them as he passed by ... and all of them were healed' (Acts 5:12–15).

However, some people who were not apostles also performed signs and wonders (Acts 6:8; 8:6).

God's stamp of approval

I think the best way of thinking about signs and wonders is that they act like God's stamp of approval. They prove the authenticity of the person and his or her message. We see this in some descriptions where we are told that signs and wonders 'accredited' someone, or that God 'confirmed' his message with such miracles (Acts 2:22; 14:3; compare Hebrews 2:3–4). This is why Paul refers to signs and wonders as one of the marks of an apostle (2 Corinthians 12:12). They are something you should expect an apostle to have because the apostles were God's authorized spokesmen.

When people call at your house to check the electricity meter, they should be carrying an identity card of some kind. They should show it to you to confirm who they are; that card accredits them as official representatives of the electricity company.

So with sign and wonders. Moses, Elijah, Jesus and the apostles are accredited by signs and wonders. They are given power by the Holy Spirit to show they are from God. For example, Peter says of Jesus: 'God anointed Jesus of Nazareth with the Holy Spirit and power, and ... he went around doing good and healing all who were under the power of the devil' (Acts 10:38).

Now when someone knocks on my door and says he's there to read the meter, I can demand that he show me proof of his identity. But it doesn't work quite the same way with signs and wonders. The miracles do provide evidence, but Jesus refused to perform signs on demand for those who wanted them (Matthew

16:1-4). Similarly, Paul said that some people looked for signs, and others looked for clever arguments, but he would preach only Christ crucified to both (1 Corinthians 1:22-24; 2:1-5). It seems that God gives plenty of authentication, except to those whose attitude is wrong and who demand it from him. Ultimately our faith must be in the power of the gospel that he speaks to us, not in a miracle we've seen or a clever argument we've heard (1 Corinthians 2:4-5).

The Spirit and signs and wonders today?

There is one very clear way in which we expect the Spirit to use signs and wonders today. That is, we look back to the signs and wonders performed by Jesus and the apostles and so know that they bear God's stamp of approval. John tells us that this is why he has written his gospel: he has told us about the signs Jesus performed so that we will know who Jesus is and believe in him (John 20:30-31). So we, too, should point people back to those signs and wonders that are recorded for us and tell them the significance of them.

This is what the apostles themselves did in verses we've quoted above from Acts. They said Jesus was accredited by God, and that God had pointed Jesus out. Supremely he has done so in *the* sign and *the* wonder, the resurrection. Similarly, we should say that we can trust what the apostles say because they too have been pointed out by God.

But should signs and wonders continue today as part of everyone's ongoing evangelism? John Wimber thought they should; he referred to 'doing the stuff', meaning performing miracles. I don't think so. There aren't many parts of the New Testament letters that talk about evangelism, but those that do so remain completely silent about performing miracles. Rather, the focus is on our words to people (see, for example, Colossians 4:2-6; 1 Peter 3:15-16). Also, the letters to pastors like Timothy and Titus, which tell them how to go about their ministry, don't mention a word about signs and wonders. Again, the focus is on their teaching ministry. The understanding seems to be that God confirmed his acts of salvation and his message of salvation with such signs, and then later generations look back to those events, rather than that God repeatedly confirms his message in each new generation.

Now, having said that, there are many reports from around the world and through history in which God has clearly worked in miraculous ways. Sometimes it was a moment of supernatural protection, sometimes a miraculous healing, often in missionary contexts. And these miracles have functioned to bring people to see that God is behind the gospel and those speaking it. So this does happen today. But at the same time we must remember that on many occasions there hasn't been miraculous protection and there hasn't been answered prayer for healing. There have even been examples where the local witch-doctor has been able to perform a healing and the missionary hasn't.

So we certainly shouldn't say that God never does such things today. But I do think there is a clear difference between the time of the apostles and now. The difference lies in our *expectation*. It seems that Paul and Peter knew they could walk down the street and heal whomever they met. They could have walked into the local hospital and cleared it out. Actually, nobody claims to be able to do that today – not even at the healing meetings. But neither is it the case that we never expect God ever to do anything miraculous again. So we press on in speaking the gospel, looking to God to empower us and guide us by his Spirit. He may on occasion choose to confirm our words in miraculous ways. But I think the Bible leads us to think that that will be the exception rather than the rule.

Remember that seminar on evangelism I mentioned at the start of this chapter? We admitted to each other that we were scared. We went on to remind each other that those who told us the gospel did so 'by the Holy Spirit sent from heaven' (1 Peter 1:12). We prayed that the Spirit would empower us to do the same.

study 9

There is no one passage that speaks directly about this. Rather, we will survey a variety of passages in Acts.

Read Acts 1:6–8

1. What is the disciples' concern at this point? How does Jesus answer it?
2. What is Jesus' master plan for the future? In what way is the Holy Spirit the key to it?
3. Is this promise of 'power' true for us in exactly the same way as for the apostles?

Read Acts 4:8, 31

4. Look at the context and think how Peter may have been feeling at this point. Why does Luke specifically mention that he is 'filled' with the Spirit here?
5. What result does being filled with the Spirit have in verse 31? How does this fit with what the believers have just been praying?
6. What would being filled with the Spirit look like for us? Discuss some real examples in which you feel the need of 'boldness' in speaking the Word of God.

Read Acts 13:1–3

7. What is the significance of the fact that the Holy Spirit was behind the first missionary journey?
8. Even if the Holy Spirit doesn't tell us who should be missionaries, what should we expect him to do with regard to mission and evangelism?
9. What will experiencing the Spirit mean from these passages?

10: The Spirit and the future

Let me tell you about Simon (not his real name, to avoid any embarrassment). Simon is schizophrenic and as a result he struggles in a number of ways. He and I used to meet regularly to chat. One conversation we had sticks in my mind. We were walking across a park and talking about healing. He'd heard the range of views on healing today – from 'Have enough faith and you'll get it' through to 'Don't even ask'.

He had a pretty good balance, I thought; that was, he thought he should ask but be prepared to live with the answer 'no'. And he had asked for healing from his schizophrenia, and many others had asked on his behalf. But the schizophrenia remained. 'I don't think God is going to heal me,' he said in the park. 'I've accepted that.' And then he paused, and the shadow of a smile passed across his face. 'But he'll heal me in heaven,' he said. 'I'm looking forward to that.'

I don't see Simon very often nowadays but I did see him again recently. I asked how he was doing.

'Same old problems,' he said. 'The voices in my head are sometimes really bad. Sometimes they tell me not to trust God, not to believe the gospel.'

I can't imagine what that must be like, and I said how sorry I was, and tried to sympathize with him over how hard that must be. I can't remember his precise words in reply, but that shadow of a smile appeared again and he said something like, 'At those times I just have to trust I belong to God and he won't let me go – that's a real comfort to me.'

And, once again, I was encouraged by Simon.

We've been thinking about the person and work of the Holy Spirit, and as we draw to an end I want us to think about the Spirit and the future. It might not strike you as a very obvious combination of topics – 'What *has* the Spirit got to do with the future?', you might be thinking. Well, as it happens, he's got an awful lot to do with it. I began by telling you about Simon because I think the Holy Spirit and the future teaches us about *hope*, and about *assurance*.

There are three images the New Testament gives us that relate to this – the Spirit as a seal, the Spirit as a down payment, and the Spirit as the firstfruits. We'll look through each in turn.

God's stamp of ownership on us

The idea of being sealed with the Spirit comes three times in Paul's letters. Here is the one from Ephesians 1:13–14:

> And you also were included in Christ when you heard the
> word of truth, the gospel of your salvation. When you
> believed, you were marked in him with a seal, the promised
> Holy Spirit, who is a deposit guaranteeing our inheritance
> until the redemption of those who are God's possession –
> to the praise of his glory.

Paul is talking about people becoming Christians. Do you see that he talks about hearing the word of truth, that is the gospel, and believing? And he says that something significant happened at that moment: when you believed you were marked in him with a seal, the promised Holy Spirit.

In Paul's day, if you sent a letter to someone, you'd melt some wax and drip some on the folded letter and then use a ring or stamp to make an imprint on it. That 'sealed' the letter and confirmed it was from you. Or if you had cattle or horses, you might brand them with your seal so that people knew that those were your cattle. In fact, they did the same with slaves to mark out whom they belonged to. The seal marks ownership. We have been sealed as people belonging to God. And that mark or seal is the Holy Spirit himself. You are sealed with the Spirit.

So this idea of being sealed by the Spirit tells us, first, about *ownership*: we belong to God.

Don't doubt it

Paul's aim for his Ephesian readers is to reassure them that they really do belong to God. Many of his readers were tempted to doubt that fact, because they were Gentiles. They knew they weren't part of God's people in the Old Testament; they weren't Jews. And a major theme in Ephesians is how Gentiles have become, with Jews, full members of the people of God, with no remaining difference between them (see, for example, 2:11–22). In this passage Paul is reassuring them about this: you too were included in Christ, he says; you were marked as belonging to God.

Today, of course, we're not tempted to doubt our status before God because we're not Jews – such an idea wouldn't even occur to us. However, we can be tempted for a variety of other reasons. It might be that we haven't had an experience that other Christians speak of having. Or it might be because we still struggle with sin in our lives. Or it might be because sometimes our faith just doesn't seem very real, or at least not as real as it seems to be for others.

In fact, at some points in history this very idea of being 'sealed' has actually been a source of insecurity for Christians. People have spoken of it as a later experience that you need to seek, with the resultant teaching that some Christians are sealed and others aren't. Inevitably, then, people ask themselves, 'Am I sealed by the Spirit?'

But when does Paul say you are sealed, in this passage? Verse 13 says it is 'when you believed' the gospel. When you believed in Jesus you were sealed. On the other occasions when Paul mentions being sealed, he does so assuming that every Christian is sealed. For example, in Ephesians 4:30 he says, 'Do not grieve the Holy Spirit of God, with whom you were sealed for the day of redemption.' In giving that command he assumes that every Christian reading the letter is sealed.

This is reassurance – Paul is saying that you really do belong to God. God *did* put his stamp of ownership on you when you trusted Christ, and he will keep you safe. If you have believed the gospel, then God has said 'Mine' over you, just as much as over anyone else. And so once again we see that there are no second-class Christians.

We need to recognize that our different personalities play a part here. Some of us are more confident in ourselves (should we say 'over-confident' or 'proud'?), and we don't doubt that we belong to God. In fact it never really occurs to us as a possibility! Others of us, though, are less sure of ourselves and can easily live the Christian life thinking that God is still making up his mind about us.

My wife tells me that I was a terrible boyfriend – in a number of ways. One of the main ones was that for her it felt as if I was perpetually making my mind up about her – weighing up how I felt, asking myself, 'Do I really like her, or don't I'? I'd like to defend myself, of course, and say that uncertainty is just an inevitable part of going out with someone. But I can believe I wasn't great at communicating commitment as well.

Similarly, some of us can feel as if God is weighing us up, watching to see what we'll do next before he makes a final decision about us. Being sealed by the Spirit tells us the very opposite. God wants us to know that he *has* made his mind up about us, and so he has sealed us with his Spirit. God has made his promise; he's said, 'I take you to be my people'; he's sealed it and it's definite. In thinking about our relationship with him, we should know that God wants us to enjoy that security, that assurance that we are his and he is committed to us. He doesn't want us living life as nervous Christians.

Sealed for the future

There is actually some Old Testament background to this idea of being sealed or marked out as God's people. It comes in Ezekiel 9, where Ezekiel has a vision of God's judgment that is about to come on Jerusalem. But we're told that before that judgment arrives God sends someone through the city to put a mark on the forehead of those who grieve over the evil of the city. These are the people who've remained faithful to God. They are marked out, and then when the judgment comes they are kept safe from it. There's a very similar picture given in Revelation 7, again of God's people being marked as his and being kept safe.

And so, while the focus of this image of a seal that Paul uses is on ownership, it also tells us about *protection*. In fact, in Ephesians 1 it clearly has a sense of being kept safe for the future. In the verses from Ephesians 1, above, we read about the 'redemption of those who are God's possession'. That is the final salvation of those who belong to God. In Ephesians 4:30 we read about being 'sealed for the day of redemption'. This 'sealing' is marking us out as God's until he does something else, keeping us safe until that day ahead. In this sense it is closely linked with the next image we'll look at – the down payment.

God's down payment on us

The second image to look at is the Spirit as a deposit or a down payment. There are two passages where this is linked with the idea of the seal we've just looked at.

Having believed, you were marked in him with a seal, the promised Holy Spirit, who is a deposit guaranteeing our inheritance until the redemption of those who are God's possession – to the praise of his glory.
(Ephesians 1:13–14)

Now it is God who makes both us and you stand firm in Christ. He anointed us, set his seal of ownership on us, and put his Spirit in our hearts as a deposit, guaranteeing what is to come.
(2 Corinthians 1:21–22)

If you want to buy a house, and you can't buy it outright, you put down a down payment, or a deposit. It is part of the purchase price itself, but it mainly acts to reassure the seller that you're serious. You wouldn't put down that sort of money if you weren't going to go the whole way and buy it.

That's exactly the meaning of the word Paul uses here. God puts his Spirit in us, as a deposit, the down payment that guarantees that the rest is to come. That's why in Ephesians it is followed by mention of the future: 'guaranteeing our inheritance until the redemption of those who are God's possession'. The Spirit acts as a down payment that guarantees the inheritance God has stored up for us in the future.

Remember what's to come

This points us to something we easily forget about being a Christian: God hasn't finished yet. In fact, God is only halfway through with his plans. Or, to use the language above, God has paid only the down payment – he hasn't completed the deal yet.

It's easiest to see this with some examples. So here in Ephesians 1 it says we have a guarantee until the redemption of those who are God's possession. But aren't we redeemed already? In fact, earlier in chapter 1 Paul said we already had redemption (1:7). The answer to whether we are redeemed now is actually 'yes' and 'no'. I am redeemed already, that is, set free from Satan and sin, but not completely – there is a final redemption to come.

Or take the idea of adoption. We saw in an earlier chapter that we are adopted as God's children by the Spirit now (Romans 8:15). But Romans 8:23 says we still wait for our final adoption. Again, it is true now, but it is not complete; there is more to come.

Or take the idea of having new life. We are already new creations by the Spirit (2 Corinthians 5:17), and yet we have to wait for the day when God will transform our entire body, re-creating all of us to be like Christ (Philippians 3:21). There is more new-creation stuff to come. We see an example of this in 2 Corinthians 5 where Paul is talking about waiting for our heavenly bodies, and he mentions the Spirit as a deposit again:

> For while we are in this tent, we groan and are burdened, because we do not wish to be unclothed but to be clothed with our heavenly dwelling, so that what is mortal may be swallowed up by life. Now it is God who has made us for this very purpose and has given us the Spirit as a deposit, guaranteeing what is to come.
> (2 Corinthians 5:4–5)

Paul says that while we are in this 'tent' – that's our current bodies – we groan, waiting for our heavenly dwelling – that's our new, eternal bodies. And he says that God, who made us for that purpose of a heavenly body, has given us the Spirit as a down payment or deposit guaranteeing what is to come. God gives us the Spirit to guarantee that he will finish this job of re-creation.

So this talk of down payments and guaranteeing the future tells us to remember that there's more to come. God's work has started but it's not complete. The Bible often sums that up with the word 'inheritance', just as it does here in Ephesians 1:14. We have to wait to inherit all that God has planned. He has laid up more for us to come.

Being sure of what's to come

So God's work is only half done, and part of the Christian life is now waiting for the future. But the key thing to see about this idea of the Spirit as a down payment is that that future is guaranteed. The deposit has been paid and so we can be sure that God will go through with the rest of the purchase.

God has paid a hefty deposit already. In fact, it's not just a hefty deposit; it's a very personal deposit. The Spirit is the deposit himself. God has given us his Spirit – and all the work of the Spirit we've been thinking about in this book. And that reassures us for the future. My adoption by the Spirit will be completed one day because it's already begun now; my redemption will be final, because God has already started it. The gift of the Spirit means we can be sure of the future.

The first part of the harvest is in

There's another term used of the Spirit, which teaches this same point. I'll mention it more briefly because we've seen the main idea already. The Spirit is referred to in Romans 8 as the firstfruits.

> We know that the whole creation has been groaning as in the pains of childbirth right up to the present time. Not only so, but we ourselves, who have the firstfruits of the Spirit, groan inwardly as we wait eagerly for our adoption, the redemption of our bodies. For in this hope we were saved. But hope that is seen is no hope at all. Who hopes for what one already has? But if we hope for what we do not yet have, we wait for it patiently.
> (Romans 8:22–25)

The idea of 'firstfruits' is that it's the first part of the harvest which guarantees that the rest of the harvest will come. You bring it in, and it acts as a sign that says, 'More like this is on its way.'

The first part of the harvest is in, but more of the same is coming. So we have the Spirit and his work as firstfruits, which tells us that more is on the way in future.

And so Paul speaks in the verses above of 'hope'. And he points out that the very idea of hope is that we don't have everything yet – who hopes for what they already have? If we've received everything God's planned already, then our current experience is all there is; there's no more to come. Fortunately, that's not the case. We long for the completion of God's work; we long for the rest of the harvest. And so we now live waiting patiently, reassured that it will come in God's own time.

The beginning and the end

I think this is a fascinating aspect of the Holy Spirit and his work that we rarely appreciate. The Spirit begins God's work in our lives – he brings us new life, and brings us to know God and live for God and serve God now. I hope you've seen in this book that the Holy Spirit is how God works; all he does in our lives is through the Spirit.

But having the Holy Spirit in our lives is also a reminder of the end. Having the Spirit tells us that there's more to come. He is a reminder that we're a work in progress. And he thus assures us that God will finish the work.

Understanding life now

This is so important in understanding our Christian experience. It means we should expect both to rejoice in what God has done already and still to have a sense of longing for God to finish the job. There should be delight in what he has done, and a degree of frustration at what is incomplete.

We can easily think of some examples. I rejoice that I can live to please God now in walking by the Spirit, but I still fight with sin and still do sin, and long for the day when God will remove the possibility of sin. I rejoice in knowing God now by his Spirit, but I don't know him as well as I want to, and I long for the day when I shall see him face to face. I rejoice in the life of the church now as the temple of the Holy Spirit, but it is still a group far from perfection, and I long for the perfect fellowship and unity of the future.

So normal Christian experience involves rejoicing and groaning. It involves enjoying and longing. It means delighting and waiting. The Holy Spirit as a seal, as a deposit and as the firstfruits reminds us of all there is to come. And so my friend Simon was right to long for the future.

Reassurance in life now

We should not only understand life now; we should also be reassured. The Holy Spirit as a seal, a deposit and the firstfruits reminds us that God's work has started and he will finish the job. To go back to the down-payment idea, he will complete the deal; he'll go through with it. The same is true of the firstfruits picture – the rest of the harvest is guaranteed. Likewise, the seal is for the day of redemption.

This raises the old chestnut of whether Christians can ever lose their salvation. Some have argued that, while you have new life by the Spirit, if you turn against God and reject the gospel you effectively 'die' again and lose that new life. Others have said that this new life by the Spirit cannot be undone, and so if you are truly saved you are always saved.

I think the areas we've covered in this chapter point us to the second position – this new life by the Spirit is the beginning of the new creation, the down payment or the firstfruits, and so it should reassure us about the future now.

We have to note, though, that this reassurance is there only while I display the work of the Spirit. There should be no reassurance in people having prayed a prayer for salvation some years ago if they are not showing any signs of the Spirit being at work in their lives now. You may remember that in an earlier chapter we said we could resist the Spirit, and if that's what we're doing, then we have no reassurance. The Spirit at work means that I will continue to trust Jesus as Saviour and follow him as Lord; it means that I will grow in love for God and for my fellow believers; it means that I will press on in the fight against sin and give myself to serving God in the life of the church.

However, as I see these signs of the Spirit's work in me, I can be confident that I have the Holy Spirit, who is a deposit guaranteeing my inheritance. And so my confidence rests in the fact that I am God's and he is at work in me, rather than resting on how tightly I am holding on to him. And so I think my friend Simon was right to be comforted. We belong to God and he will take us home and finish his work.

The challenge in life now

As well as understanding life now, and being reassured in life now, we also need to be challenged about life now. We've said the work of the Spirit reminds us that we are a group waiting for the future. The challenge is *how* we wait.

You may know the story of Ernest Shackleton, who led an expedition to the South Pole. The trip went horribly wrong and the ship's crew ended up stranded somewhere called Elephant Island. Shackleton himself and a few others left to try to bring help. The rest stayed on Elephant Island waiting for his return. They had to wait over three months. But each day the skipper on the island would call his men to be ready for Shackleton's return *that* day. He pointed them to their future hope, to be ready for the coming rescue and to live accordingly.

We too are to wait looking forward to our rescue, and to live accordingly. That means giving ourselves to the work of the Spirit now. We've mentioned the following verse before but it shows us this point: 'And do not grieve the Holy Spirit of God, with whom you were sealed for the day of redemption' (Ephesians 4:30).

Paul's logic here is that the Holy Spirit has sealed you for the future, so don't fight against the Spirit's work in your life now.

Don't grieve him; don't cause him pain by resisting him and the work he wants to do in changing you. In other words, live out your life now as someone sealed by the Spirit for that final day, confident that it will come.

study 10

Ephesians 1:13–14

1. Glance through what Paul has been saying in the verses before this passage (verses 3–12). How do verses 13–14 fit with what has come before?
2. How do people come to be 'included in Christ' (verse 13)?
3. What does God do by his Spirit when people are included in Christ, according to verse 13?
4. What does the image of the 'seal' tell us?
5. What is the significance of the idea that the Holy Spirit is a deposit? What does he guarantee for us?
6. How does this work of the Spirit mean I should think about the future?
7. How can we help each other wait for our redemption in a 'now'-centred culture?
8. What will experiencing the Spirit look like from this passage?

Experiencing the Spirit

We began this book by asking, 'What is the Holy Spirit's role?' I warned you that this would mean covering a lot of ground, as the Holy Spirit is involved in all that God does. But let's try to summarize what we've seen and ask what experiencing the Holy Spirit looks like.

- We've seen that the Spirit brings new life by re-creating us. And so experiencing the Spirit means to be given new spiritual life, such that we can come into God's kingdom, know God and have a relationship with him.
- We've seen that the Spirit reveals to us who Jesus is. And so experiencing the Spirit means to come to know and trust in Jesus as our Saviour, who died for us, and our Lord, who rules us. More than that, the Spirit makes Jesus real to us so that we can say we *know* him.
- We've seen that the Spirit comes into our hearts so that we can relate to God the Father as *our* Father. And so experiencing the Spirit means living in that relationship, knowing God's love, trusting his promises and having the joy and comfort of speaking to him in prayer.

- We've seen that the Spirit reveals truth to us through the Bible (which he wrote through people). And so experiencing the Spirit means growing in knowledge of God's truth and being changed in our thinking and understanding through reading and reflecting on what he has written.
- We've seen that the Spirit leads us into holiness so that we grow into the image of God. And so experiencing the Spirit is to know a desire for holiness and a hatred of sin and to fight the battle against the sinful nature.
- We've seen that the Spirit baptizes us into one body of believers so as to unite us together in our common relationship with God. And so experiencing the Spirit is to live in love and unity with other Christians, no matter what differences there are between us.
- We've seen that the Spirit is the one who wants to fill us with Christ-likeness. And so experiencing the Spirit is to follow his influence to be like Christ in all of our life.
- We've seen that the Spirit draws us to believe God's Word and go God's way, and that we can resist him in this. And so experiencing the Spirit is to know that pull towards God and his truth, and away from my sinful rebellion.
- We've seen that the Spirit gives gifts for the growth of the church. And so experiencing the Spirit means serving lovingly within our church and being a source of growth and encouragement to others.
- We've seen that the Spirit empowers us for the spread of the gospel. And so experiencing the Spirit is to have a concern for those who don't know Christ and to be bold in proclaiming the gospel to them.
- We've seen that the Spirit is the first instalment of new life in us that guarantees what is to come. And so experiencing the Spirit is to be reassured of who I am in Christ, and to look to the future, when God's promises will be fulfilled.

Without the Spirit's work there would be no new birth, no knowledge of who Jesus is, no relationship with God, no Bible to read and no understanding of truth, no growth in holiness, no unity between Christians, no confidence in evangelism, and no security for the future. The Father plans his wonderful work of salvation, which is achieved through the death and resurrection of his Son, Jesus; but the Spirit is the one who *applies* that salvation to us and makes it a reality.

Experiencing the Spirit is to experience salvation both in becoming a Christian and in growing as a Christian. Experiencing the Spirit is to have God at work in us and through us for the sake of others. Experiencing the Spirit, then, is the normal Christian life. I pray that such an experience may be yours.

Since we live by the Spirit, let us keep in step with the Spirit. (Galatians 5:25).

Further reading

D. A. Carson, *Showing the Spirit: A Theological Exposition of 1 Corinthians 12 – 14* (Carlisle: Paternoster, 1995)

Gordon Fee, *God's Empowering Presence: The Holy Spirit* (Peabody: Hendrickson, 1994)

_____ *Paul, the Spirit and the People of God* (Peabody: Hendrickson, 1996)

Sinclair Ferguson, *The Holy Spirit* (Leicester: IVP, 1996)

John Goldingay (ed.), *When Christians Disagree: Signs, Wonders and Healing* (Leicester: IVP, 1989)

Michael Green, *I Believe in the Holy Spirit* (Grand Rapids, Eerdmans, 2004)

David Jackman, *Spirit of Truth: Unlocking the Bible's Teaching on the Holy Spirit* (Fearn, Ross-shire: Christian Focus Publications, 2006)

J. I. Packer, *Keep in Step with the Spirit: Finding Fullness in Our Walk with God* (Leicester, IVP, 2005)

John Stott, *Baptism and Fullness* (Leicester, IVP, 1976)

Max Turner, *The Holy Spirit and Spiritual Gifts: In the New Testament Church and Today* (Carlisle: Paternoster, 1996)